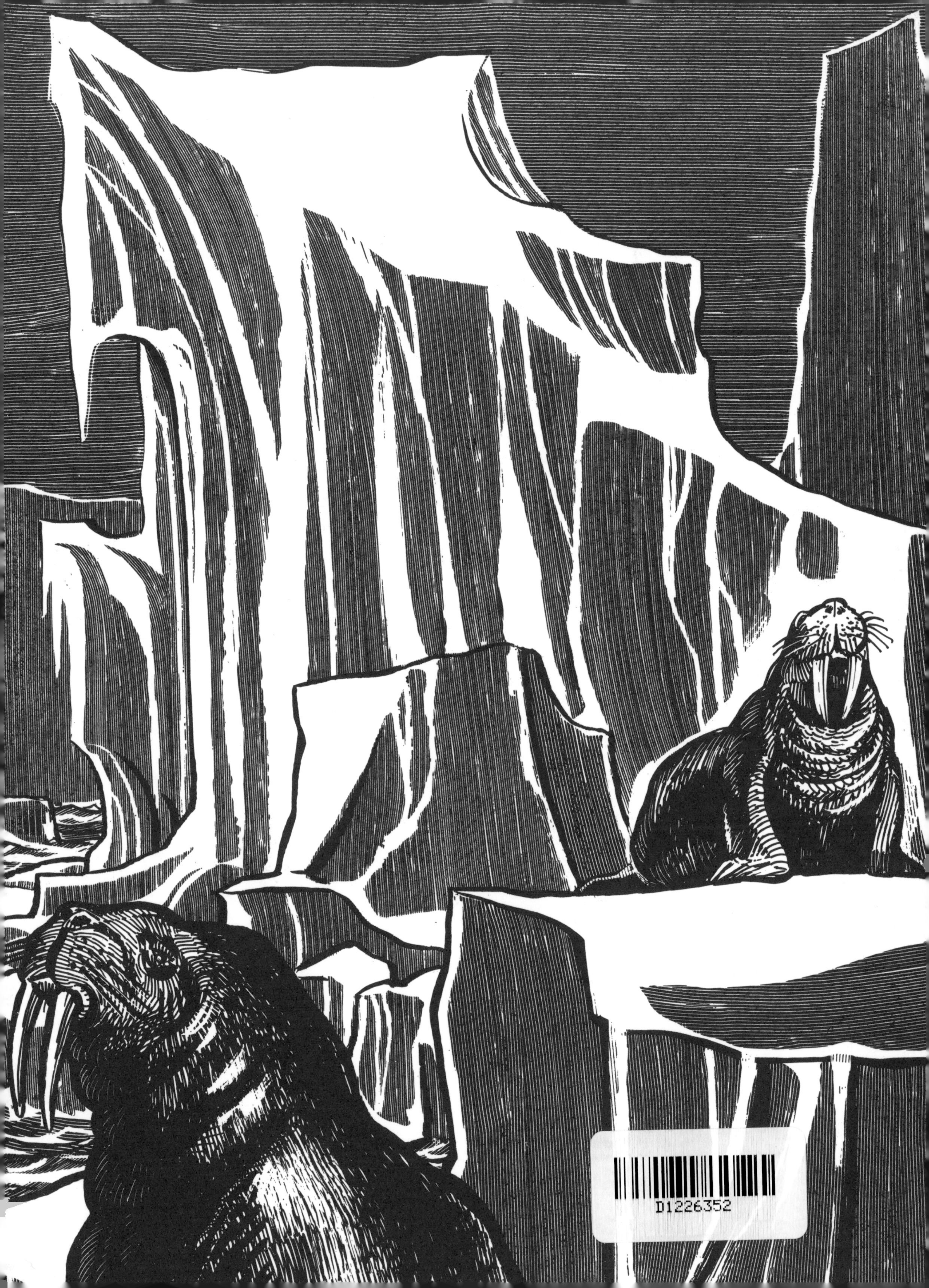

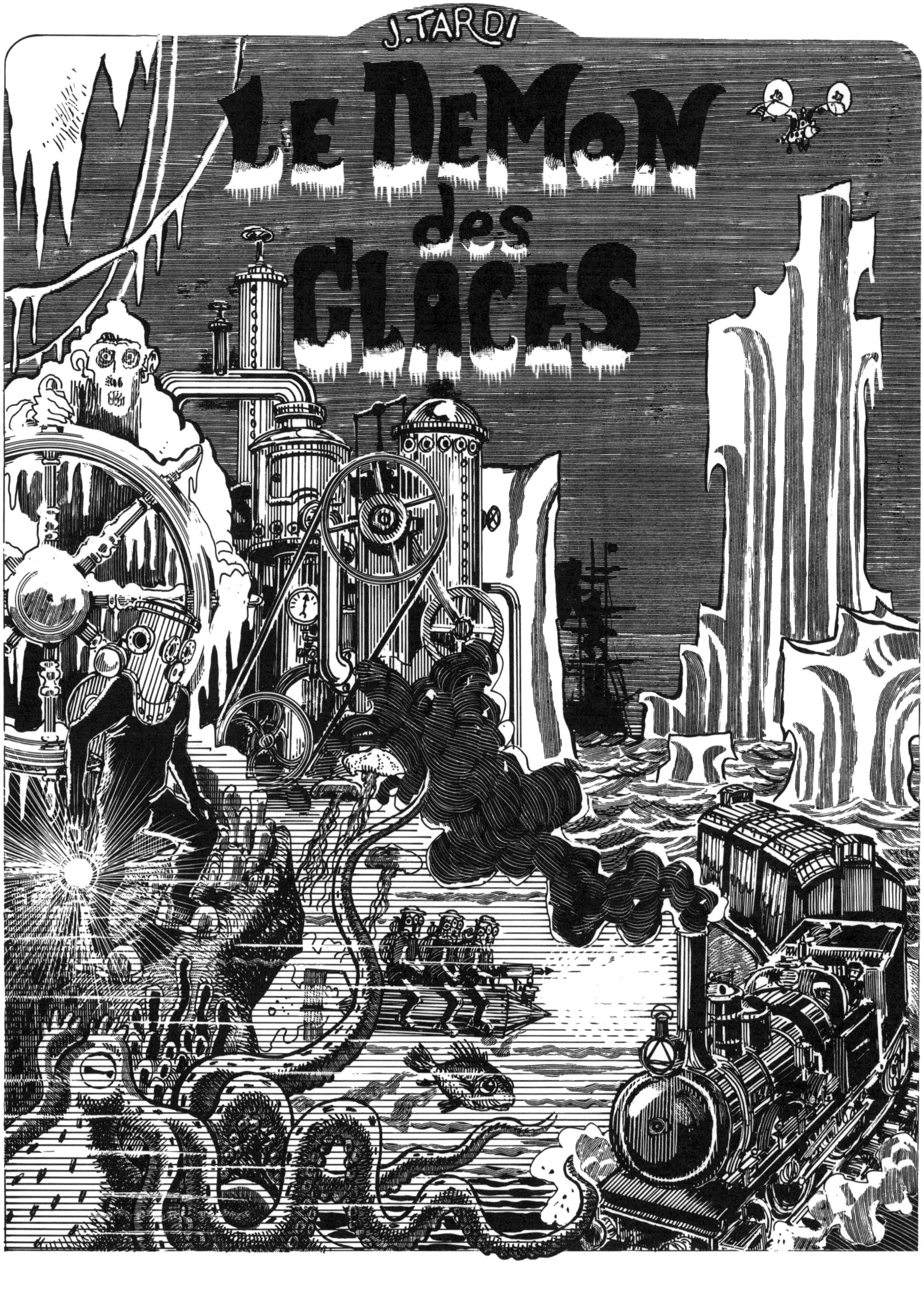
J. TARDI
LE DEMON des GLACES

THE ARCTIC MARAUDER

WRITTEN AND ILLUSTRATED BY
JACQUES TARDI

FANTAGRAPHICS BOOKS

Other books drawn by Jacques Tardi from Fantagraphics:

THE EXTRAORDINARY ADVENTURES OF ADELE BLANC-SEC Vol. 1
Written by Tardi

THE EXTRAORDINARY ADVENTURES OF ADELE BLANC-SEC Vol. 2
Written by Tardi, coming Fall 2011

IT WAS THE WAR OF THE TRENCHES
Written by Tardi

LIKE A SNIPER LINING UP HIS SHOT
Adapted by Tardi from the novel by Jean-Patrick Manchette, coming Summer 2011

WEST COAST BLUES
Adapted by Tardi from the novel by Jean-Patrick Manchette

YOU ARE THERE
Written by Jean-Claude Forest

Edited and translated by Kim Thompson. Design by Adam Grano. Production/lettering by Paul Baresh and Andrew Davis. Special calligraphy by Gavin Lees. Thanks to Chi-Wen Lee for proofreading. Associate Publisher: Eric Reynolds. Published by Gary Groth and Kim Thompson. *The Arctic Marauder* (*Le Démon des glaces*, originally published in 1974) © 2011 Editions Casterman. This edition © 2011 Fantagraphics Books. All rights reserved; permission to quote or reproduce material for reviews or notices must be obtained from Fantagraphics Books, in writing, at 7563 Lake City Way NE, Seattle, WA 98115. Visit the Fantagraphics website at www.fantagraphics. Distributed to bookstores in the U.S. by W.W. Norton and Company, Inc. (212-233-4830); distributed to comics shops in the U.S. by Diamond Comic Distributors (800-452-6642-x215); distributed in Canada by Canadian Manda Group (800-452-6642-x862). First edition: February, 2011. Printed in Singapore. ISBN 978-1-60699-435-1.

I

THE PHANTOM CLIPPER

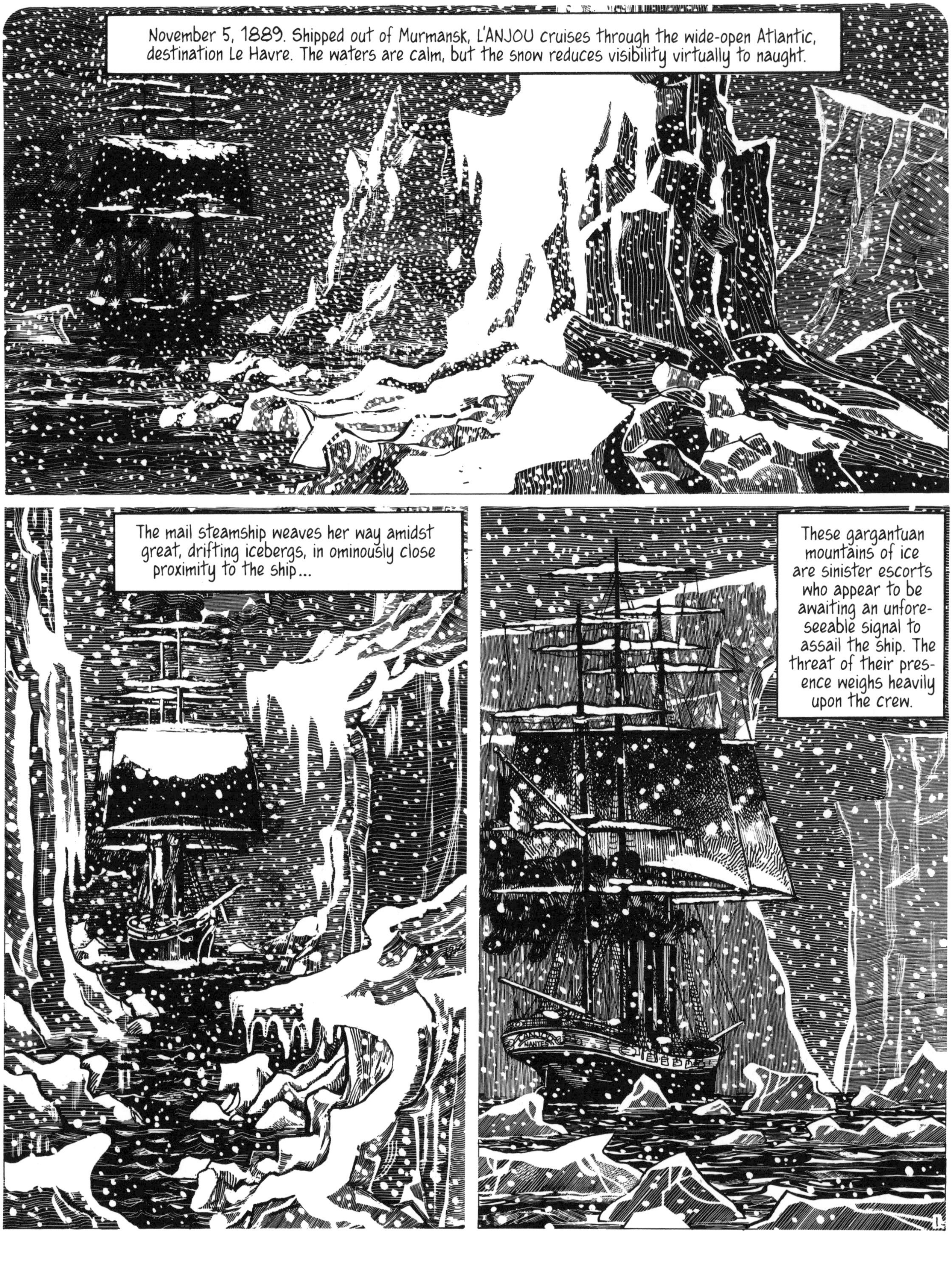
November 5, 1889. Shipped out of Murmansk, L'ANJOU cruises through the wide-open Atlantic, destination Le Havre. The waters are calm, but the snow reduces visibility virtually to naught.
The mail steamship weaves her way amidst great, drifting icebergs, in ominously close proximity to the ship...
These gargantuan mountains of ice are sinister escorts who appear to be awaiting an unforeseeable signal to assail the ship. The threat of their presence weighs heavily upon the crew.

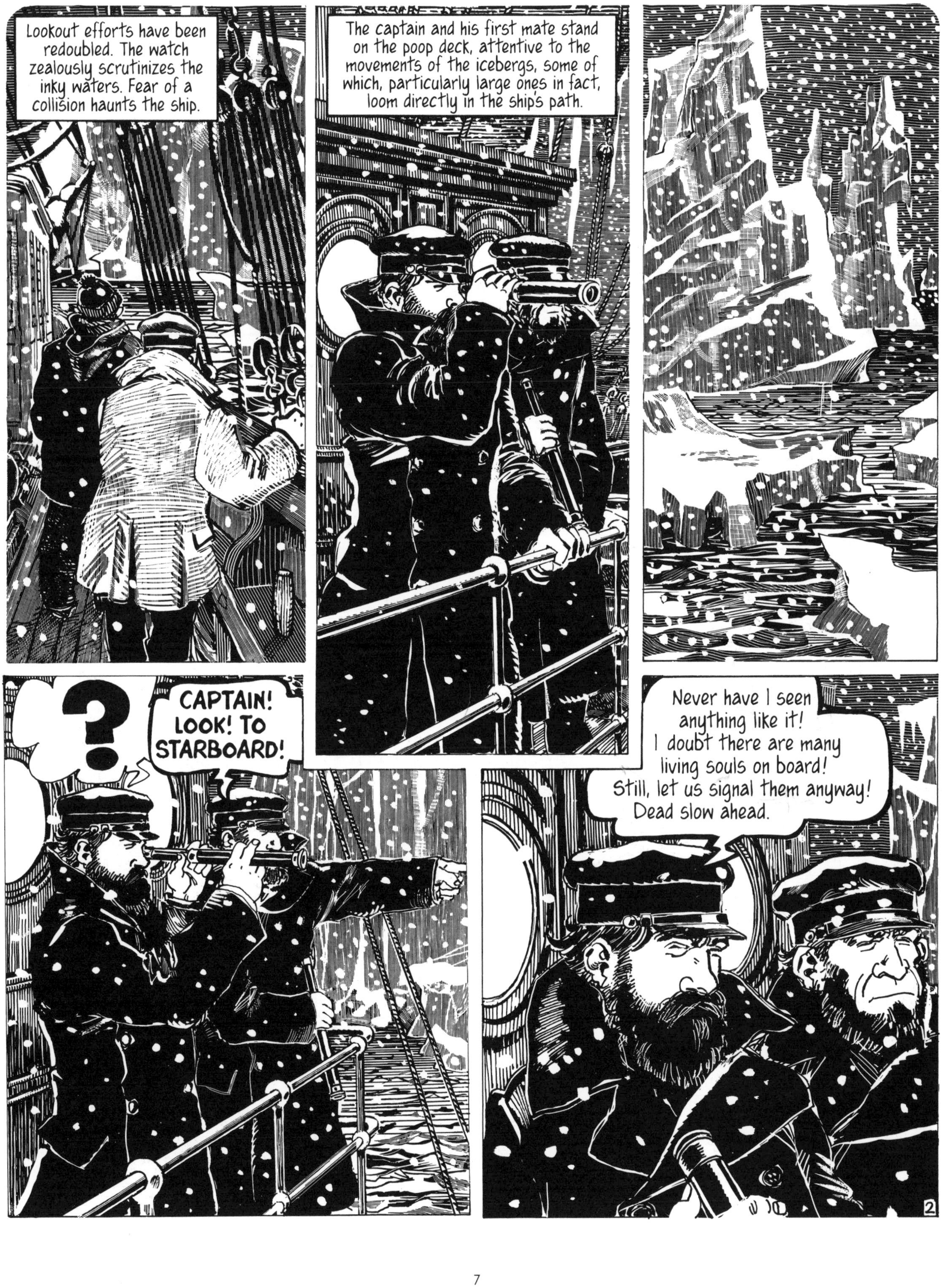
Lookout efforts have been redoubled. The watch zealously scrutinizes the inky waters. Fear of a collision haunts the ship.
The captain and his first mate stand on the poop deck, attentive to the movements of the icebergs, some of which, particularly large ones in fact, loom directly in the ship's path.
?
CAPTAIN! LOOK! TO STARBOARD!
Never have I seen anything like it! I doubt there are many living souls on board! Still, let us signal them anyway! Dead slow ahead.
2

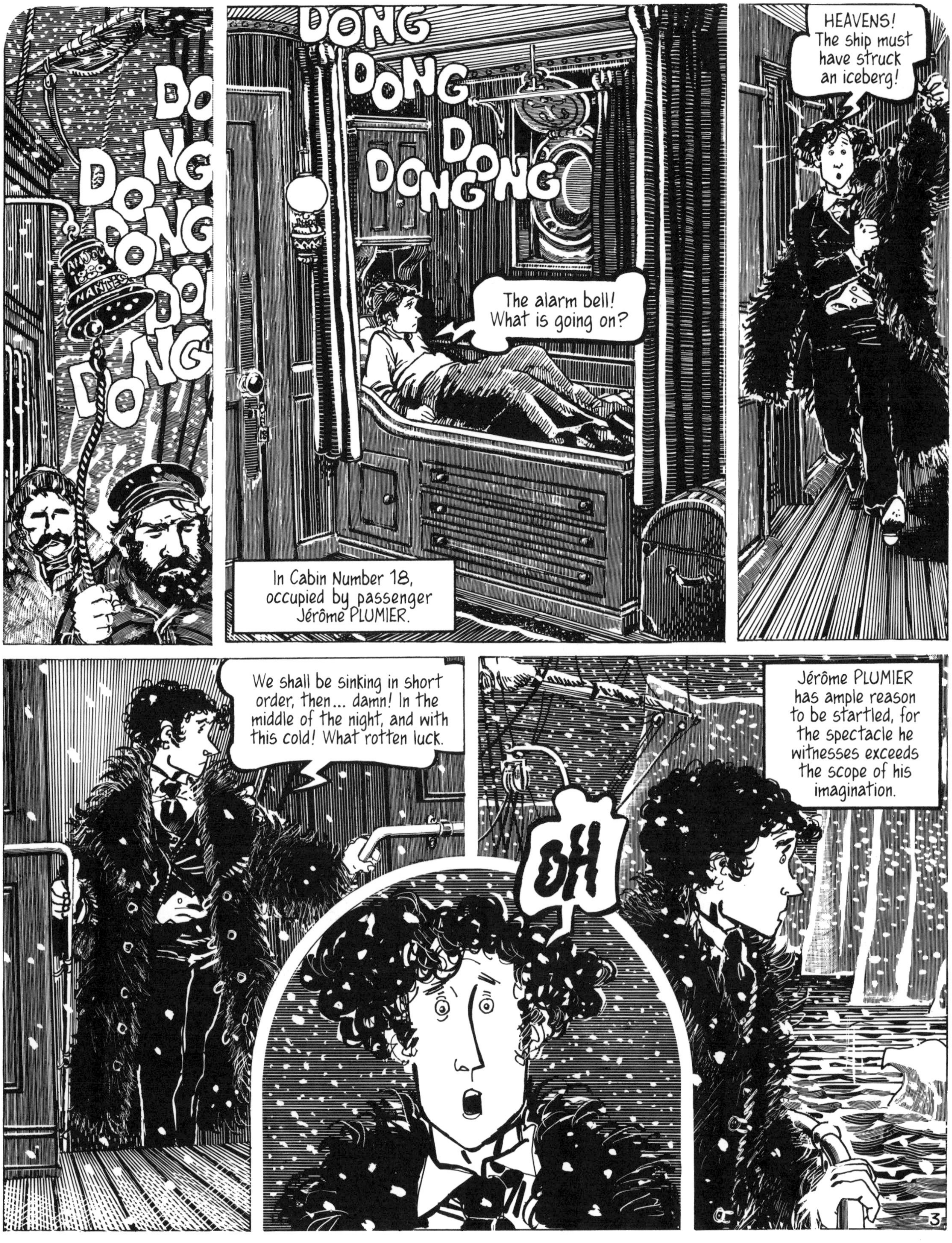
DONG DONG DONG DONG DONG
DONG DONG DONG DONG
In Cabin Number 18, occupied by passenger Jérôme PLUMIER.
The alarm bell! What is going on?
HEAVENS! The ship must have struck an iceberg!
We shall be sinking in short order, then... damn! In the middle of the night, and with this cold! What rotten luck.
Jérôme PLUMIER has ample reason to be startled, for the spectacle he witnesses exceeds the scope of his imagination.
OH
3

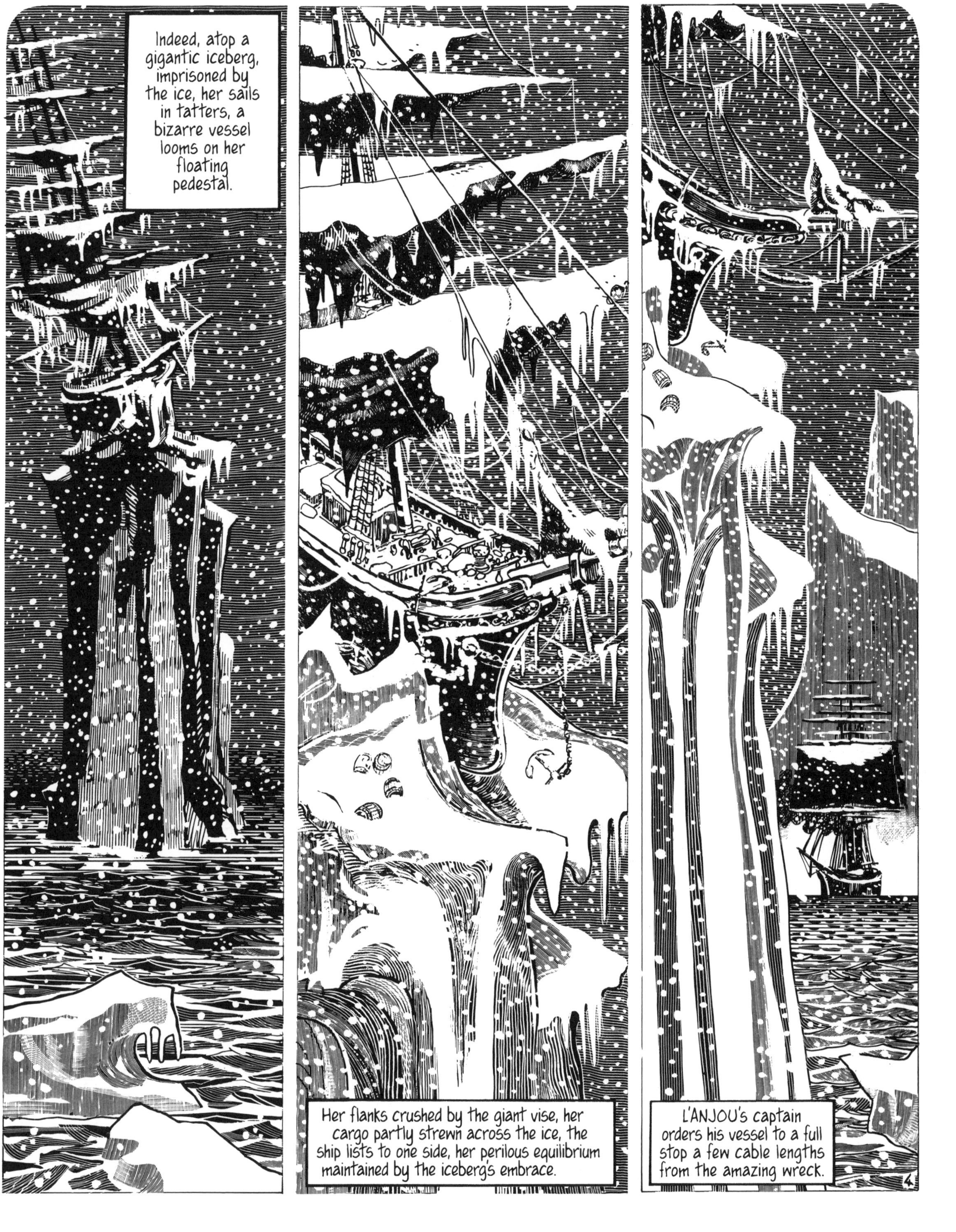
Indeed, atop a gigantic iceberg, imprisoned by the ice, her sails in tatters, a bizarre vessel looms on her floating pedestal.
Her flanks crushed by the giant vise, her cargo partly strewn across the ice, the ship lists to one side, her perilous equilibrium maintained by the iceberg's embrace.
L'ANJOU's captain orders his vessel to a full stop a few cable lengths from the amazing wreck.

Dearest, take my binoculars, this is quite a sight.

Is it a French vessel?

How did it end up there?

Quite simply! Allow me to explain...

Mind-boggling!

The passengers have surged onto the forward deck. The appearance of the ship has aroused a chorus of comment. Upon her bow the name "THE ICELAND LOAFER" can be made out.

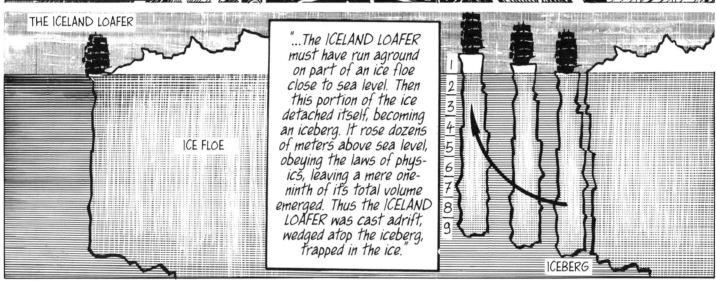

THE ICELAND LOAFER

ICE FLOE

"...The ICELAND LOAFER must have run aground on part of an ice floe close to sea level. Then this portion of the ice detached itself, becoming an iceberg. It rose dozens of meters above sea level, obeying the laws of physics, leaving a mere one-ninth of its total volume emerged. Thus the ICELAND LOAFER was cast adrift, wedged atop the iceberg, trapped in the ice."

ICEBERG

Launch a lifeboat. It is our moral obligation to visit this wreck and ascertain that there are no survivors. Make haste, this is not a safe place. These giant icebergs trouble me.

Yes Sir, Captain.

Captain! I understand you are sending a boat to the wreck. Might I find a berth on board? I am a medical student and...

Ah! Noble and generous lad! How comforting to know one may still encounter young men whose ardor burns with a hot flame in their chest. Thank you, Sir! Shake me by the hand!

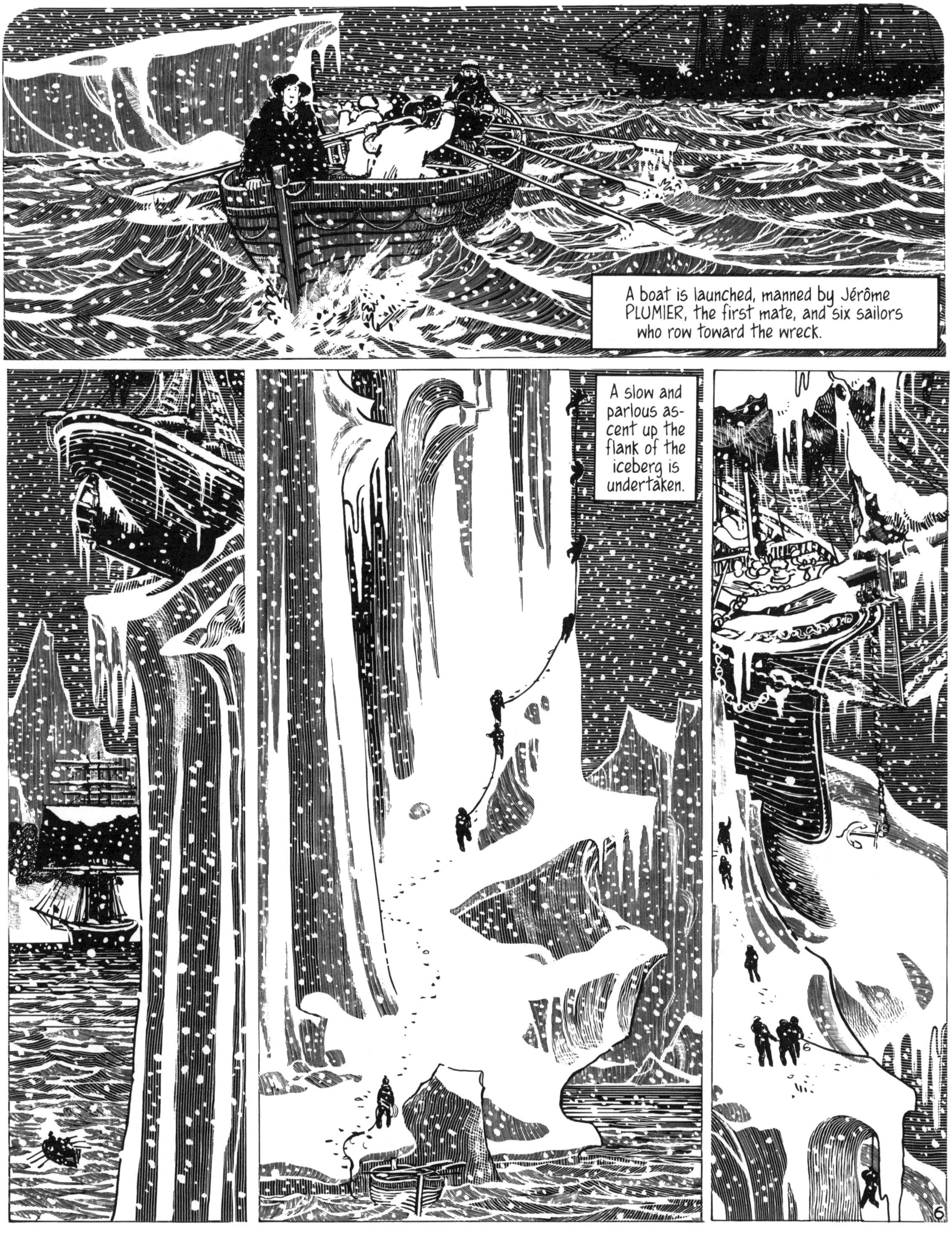
A boat is launched, manned by Jérôme PLUMIER, the first mate, and six sailors who row toward the wreck.
A slow and parlous ascent up the flank of the iceberg is undertaken.

When the crew members reach the icy deck of the ship, their surprise is boundless...

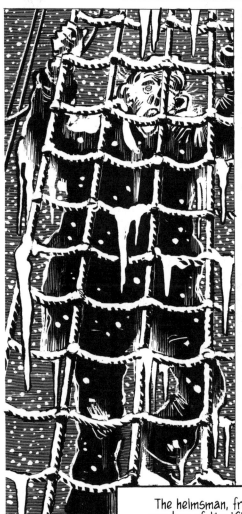

ZOUNDS! What happened here? Let us proceed below decks.

The helmsman, frozen solid, welded to his wheel, stares at the ragged sails. Every member of THE ICELAND LOAFER's crew is at his post, some in the rigging, others on the yardarms folding the sails, petrified on the deck, seized by who knows what icy breath that fell upon them, transmogrifying them into so many statues of ice.

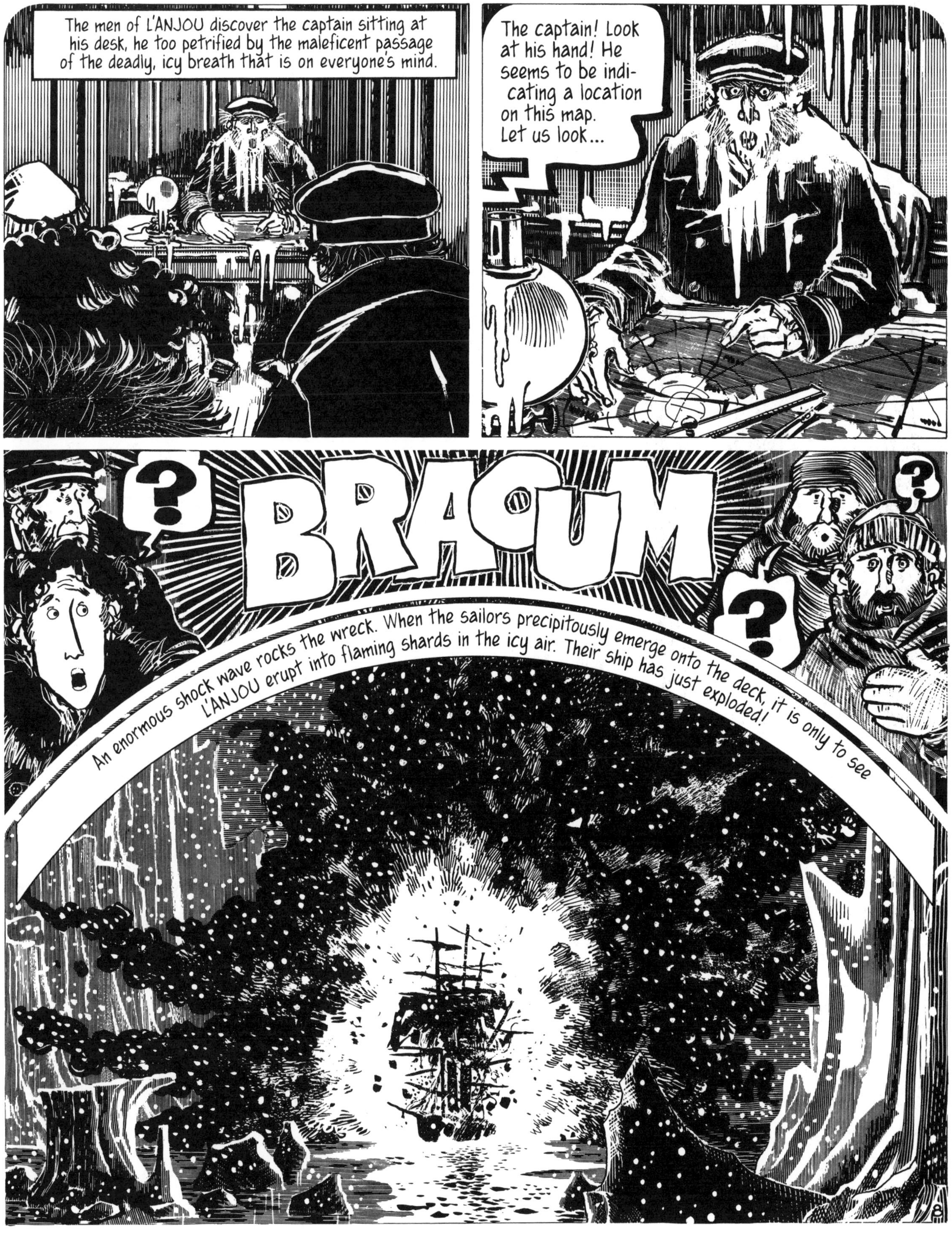

The men of L'ANJOU discover the captain sitting at his desk, he too petrified by the maleficent passage of the deadly, icy breath that is on everyone's mind.
The captain! Look at his hand! He seems to be indicating a location on this map. Let us look...
?
BRACUM
?
?
An enormous shock wave rocks the wreck. When the sailors precipitously emerge onto the deck, it is only to see L'ANJOU erupt into flaming shards in the icy air. Their ship has just exploded!

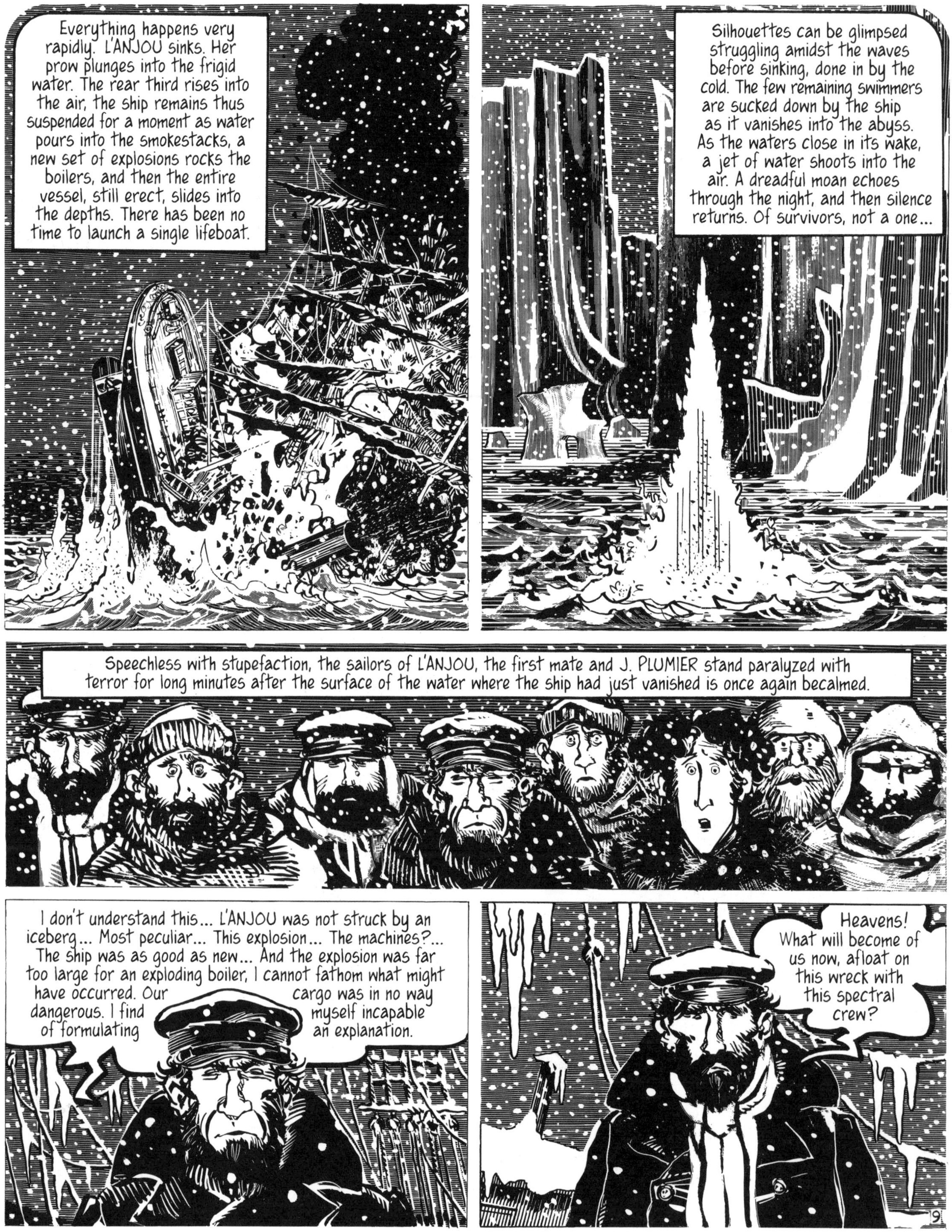
Everything happens very rapidly. L'ANJOU sinks. Her prow plunges into the frigid water. The rear third rises into the air, the ship remains thus suspended for a moment as water pours into the smokestacks, a new set of explosions rocks the boilers, and then the entire vessel, still erect, slides into the depths. There has been no time to launch a single lifeboat.
Silhouettes can be glimpsed struggling amidst the waves before sinking, done in by the cold. The few remaining swimmers are sucked down by the ship as it vanishes into the abyss. As the waters close in its wake, a jet of water shoots into the air. A dreadful moan echoes through the night, and then silence returns. Of survivors, not a one...
Speechless with stupefaction, the sailors of L'ANJOU, the first mate and J. PLUMIER stand paralyzed with terror for long minutes after the surface of the water where the ship had just vanished is once again becalmed.
I don't understand this... L'ANJOU was not struck by an iceberg... Most peculiar... This explosion... The machines?... The ship was as good as new... And the explosion was far too large for an exploding boiler, I cannot fathom what might have occurred. Our cargo was in no way dangerous. I find myself incapable of formulating an explanation.
Heavens! What will become of us now, afloat on this wreck with this spectral crew?
9

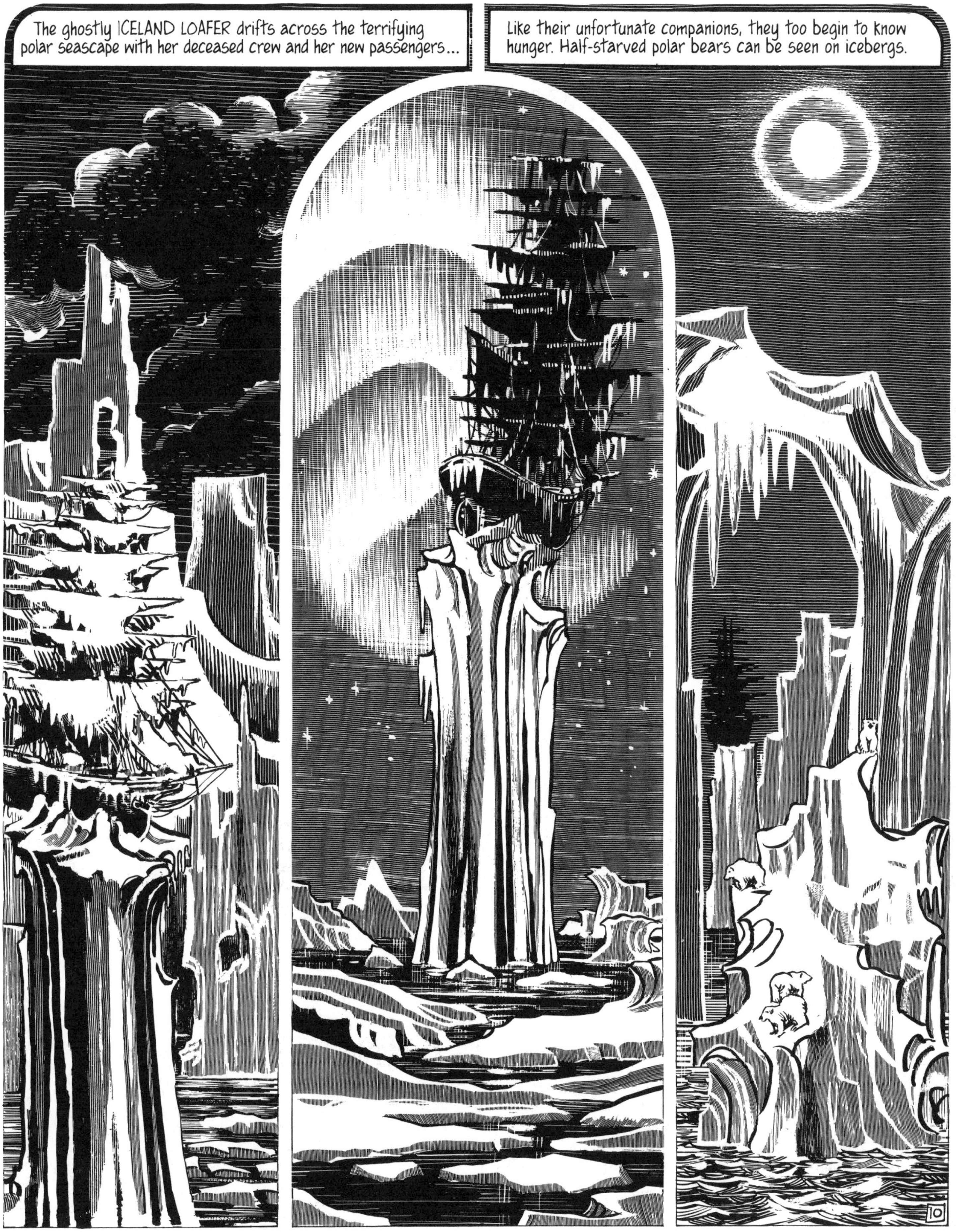
The ghostly ICELAND LOAFER drifts across the terrifying polar seascape with her deceased crew and her new passengers...
Like their unfortunate companions, they too begin to know hunger. Half-starved polar bears can be seen on icebergs.
10

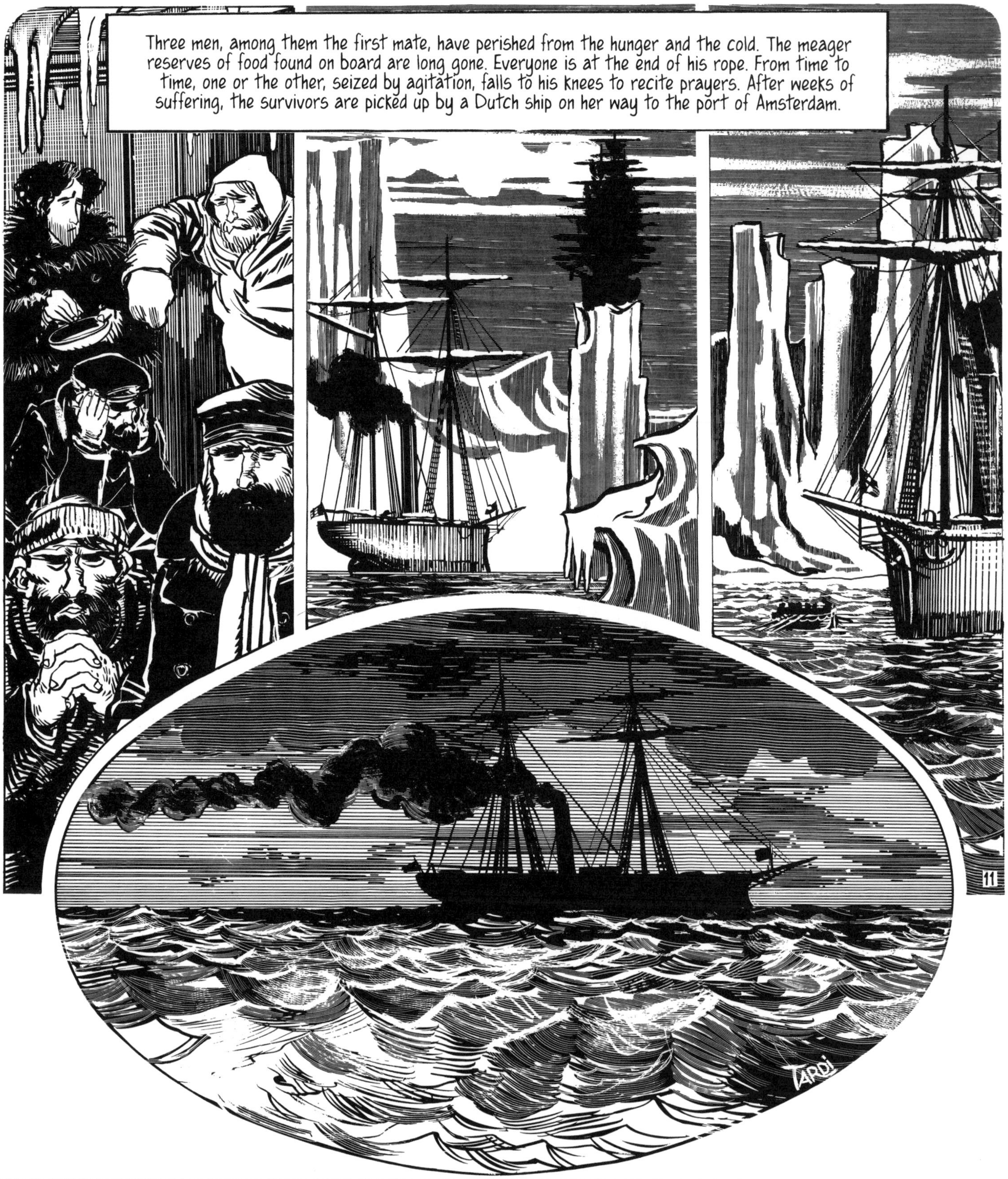
Three men, among them the first mate, have perished from the hunger and the cold. The meager reserves of food found on board are long gone. Everyone is at the end of his rope. From time to time, one or the other, seized by agitation, falls to his knees to recite prayers. After weeks of suffering, the survivors are picked up by a Dutch ship on her way to the port of Amsterdam.
11
TARDI

The escapees leave the ICELAND LOAFER to haunt the Arctic's icy solitude. Embedded atop her fateful pedestal, she carries her mystery to the depths of the boreal hell. Much intrigued, J. PLUMIER has carefully secured the map which the captain of the ICELAND LOAFER was indicating. Where was the officer pointing with his frigid digit? What is this location whose very lack of distinguishing characteristics makes it even more mystifying? What supernatural event befell the petrified crew of the grounded ship? Perhaps the solution to the mystery of the Phantom Clipper might be found in this obscure location in the heart of the ocean.

II

THE OBSEQUIES OF LOUIS-FERDINAND CHAPOUTIER

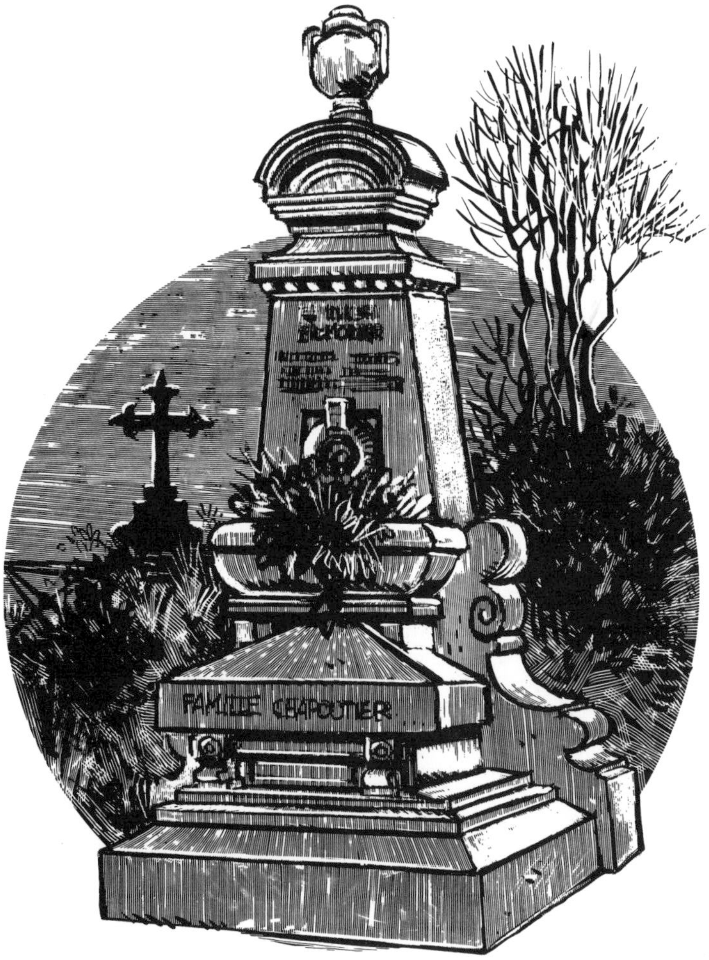
FAMILLE CHAPOUTIER

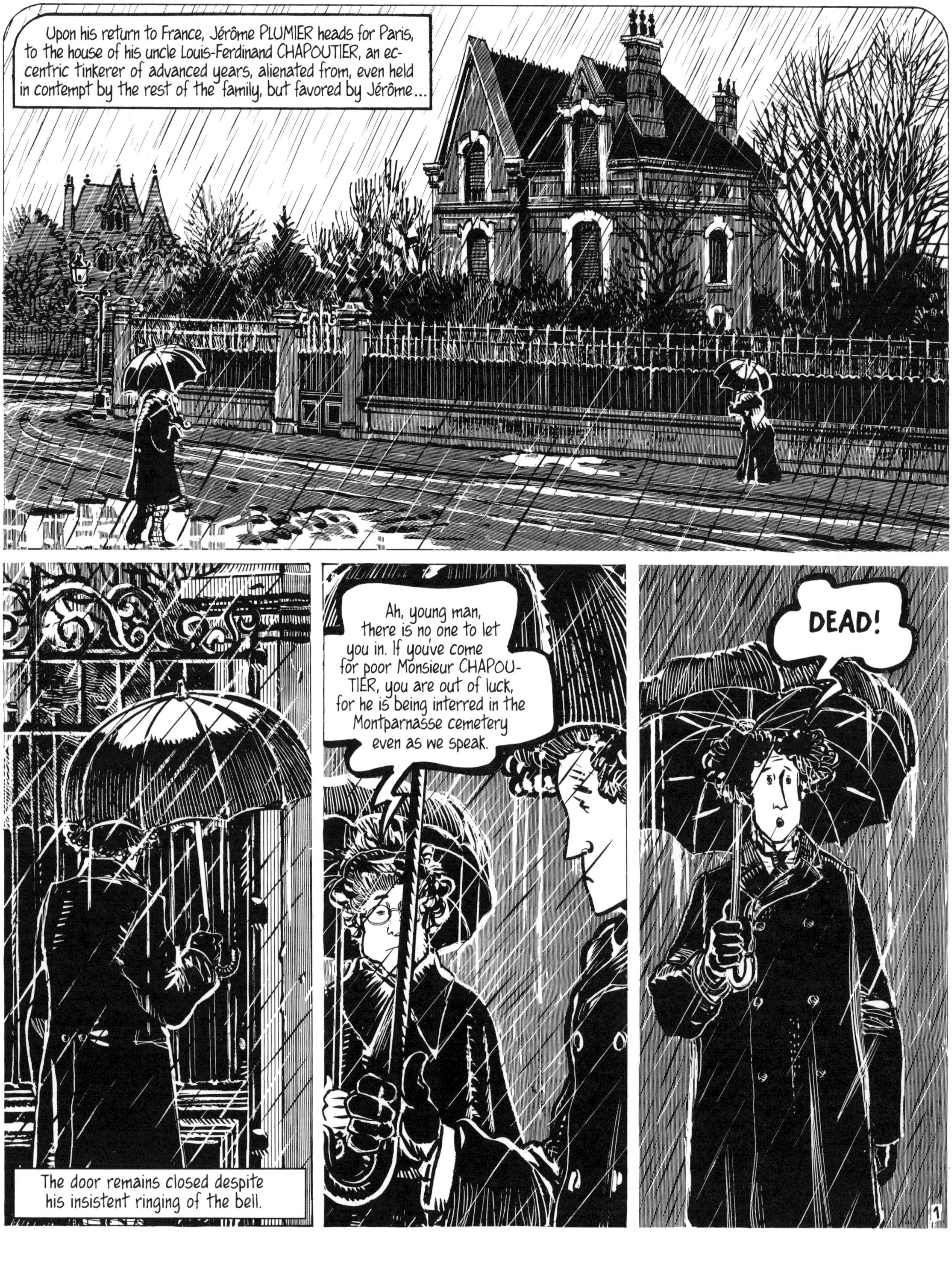
Upon his return to France, Jérôme PLUMIER heads for Paris, to the house of his uncle Louis-Ferdinand CHAPOUTIER, an eccentric tinkerer of advanced years, alienated from, even held in contempt by the rest of the family, but favored by Jérôme...
The door remains closed despite his insistent ringing of the bell.
Ah, young man, there is no one to let you in. If you've come for poor Monsieur CHAPOUTIER, you are out of luck, for he is being interred in the Montparnasse cemetery even as we speak.
DEAD!

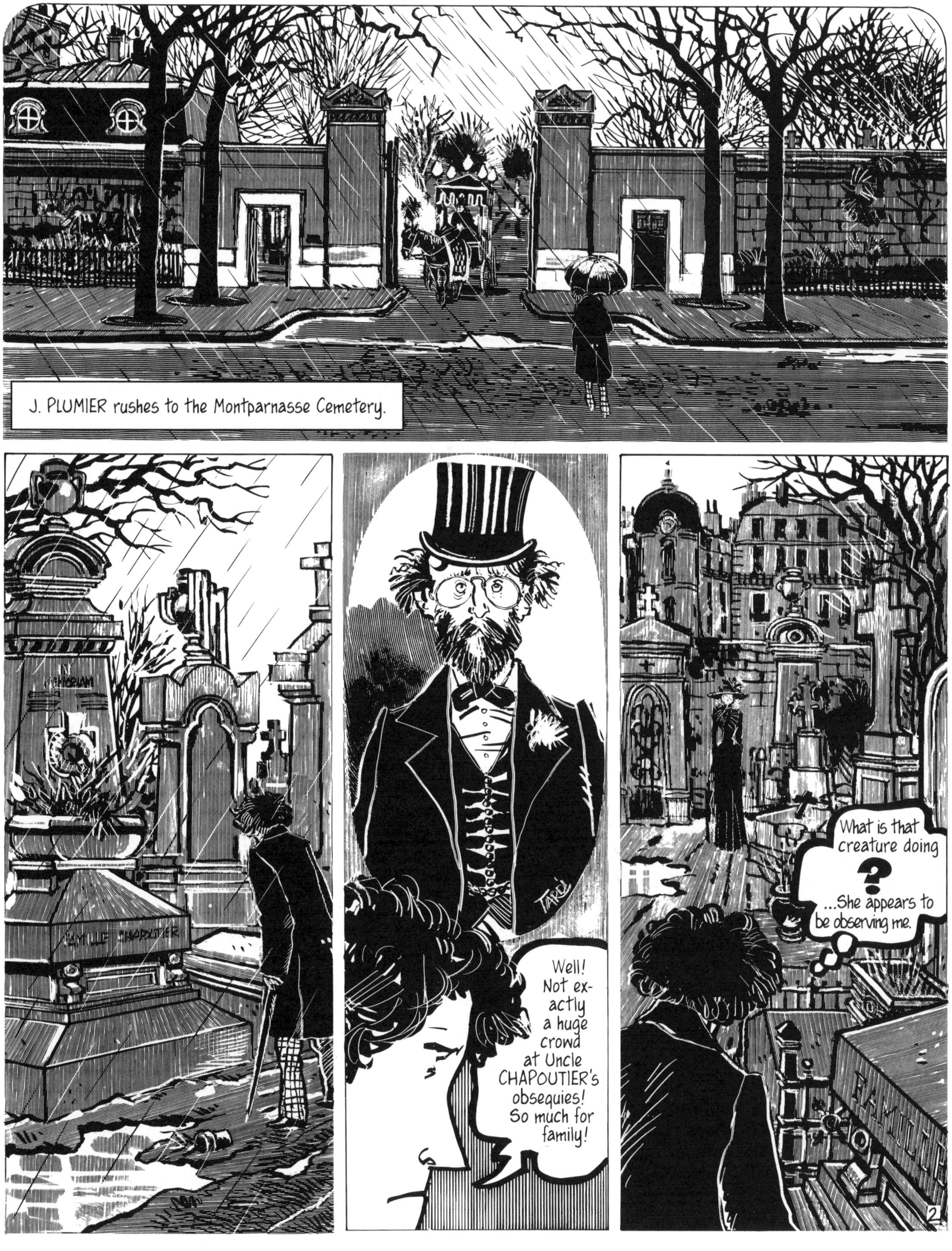
J. PLUMIER rushes to the Montparnasse Cemetery.
Well! Not exactly a huge crowd at Uncle CHAPOUTIER's obsequies! So much for family!
What is that creature doing ? ...She appears to be observing me.

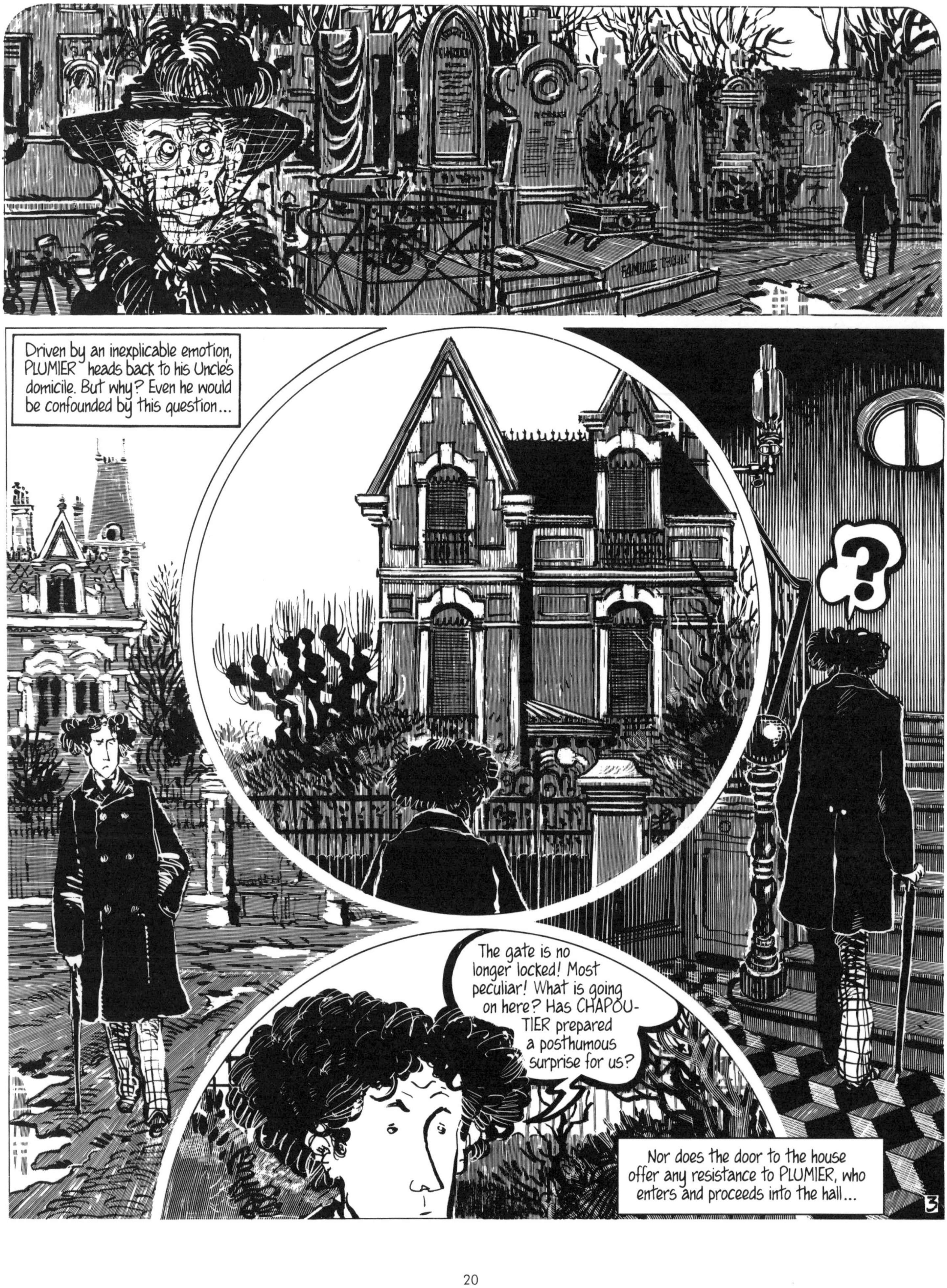
FAMILLE
Driven by an inexplicable emotion, PLUMIER heads back to his Uncle's domicile. But why? Even he would be confounded by this question...
?
The gate is no longer locked! Most peculiar! What is going on here? Has CHAPOU-TIER prepared a posthumous surprise for us?
Nor does the door to the house offer any resistance to PLUMIER, who enters and proceeds into the hall...
3

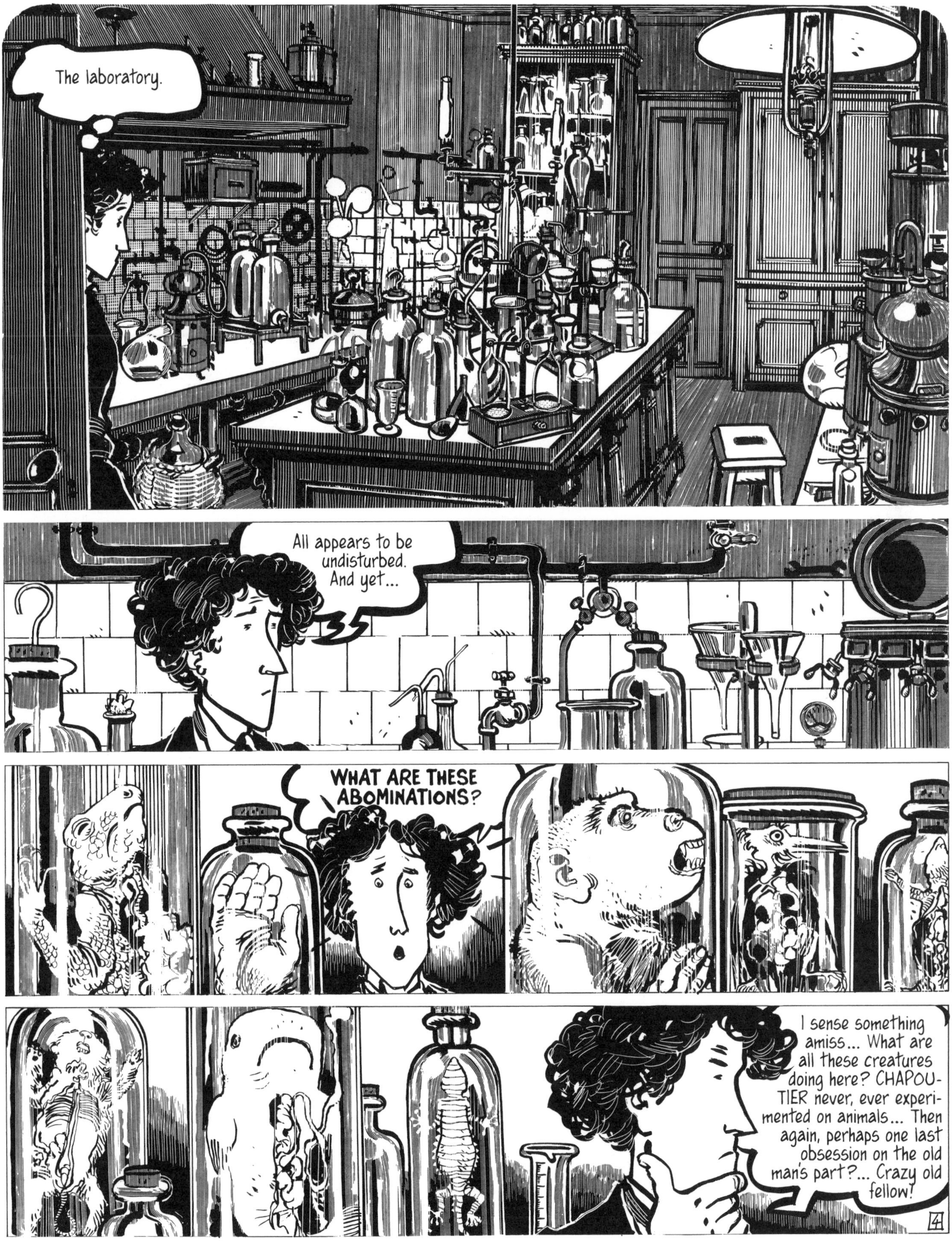

The laboratory.
All appears to be undisturbed. And yet...
WHAT ARE THESE ABOMINATIONS?
I sense something amiss... What are all these creatures doing here? CHAPOUTIER never, ever experimented on animals... Then again, perhaps one last obsession on the old man's part?... Crazy old fellow!
4

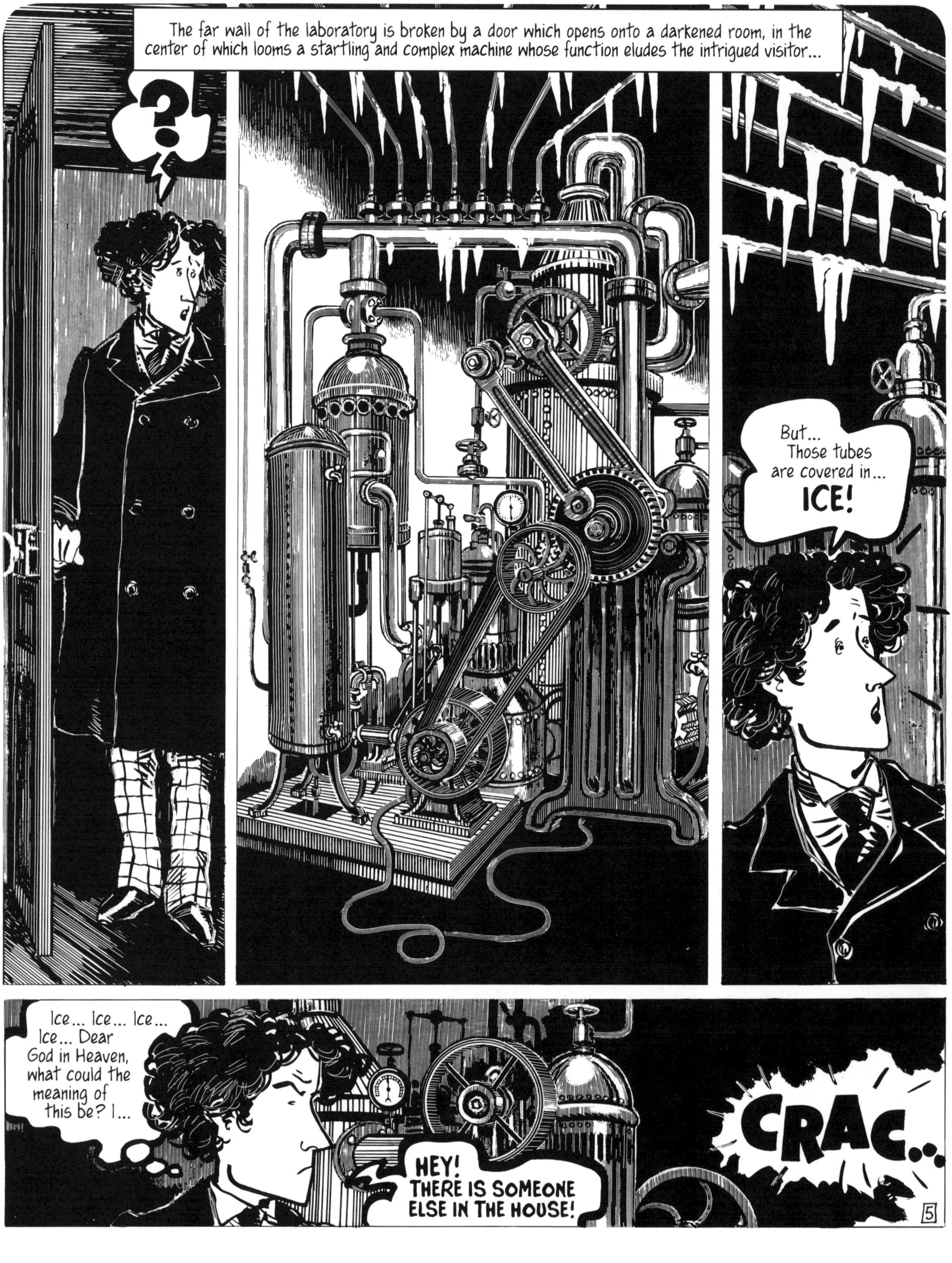

The far wall of the laboratory is broken by a door which opens onto a darkened room, in the center of which looms a startling and complex machine whose function eludes the intrigued visitor...
?
But... Those tubes are covered in... ICE!
Ice... Ice... Ice... Ice... Dear God in Heaven, what could the meaning of this be? I...
HEY! THERE IS SOMEONE ELSE IN THE HOUSE!
CRAC...
5

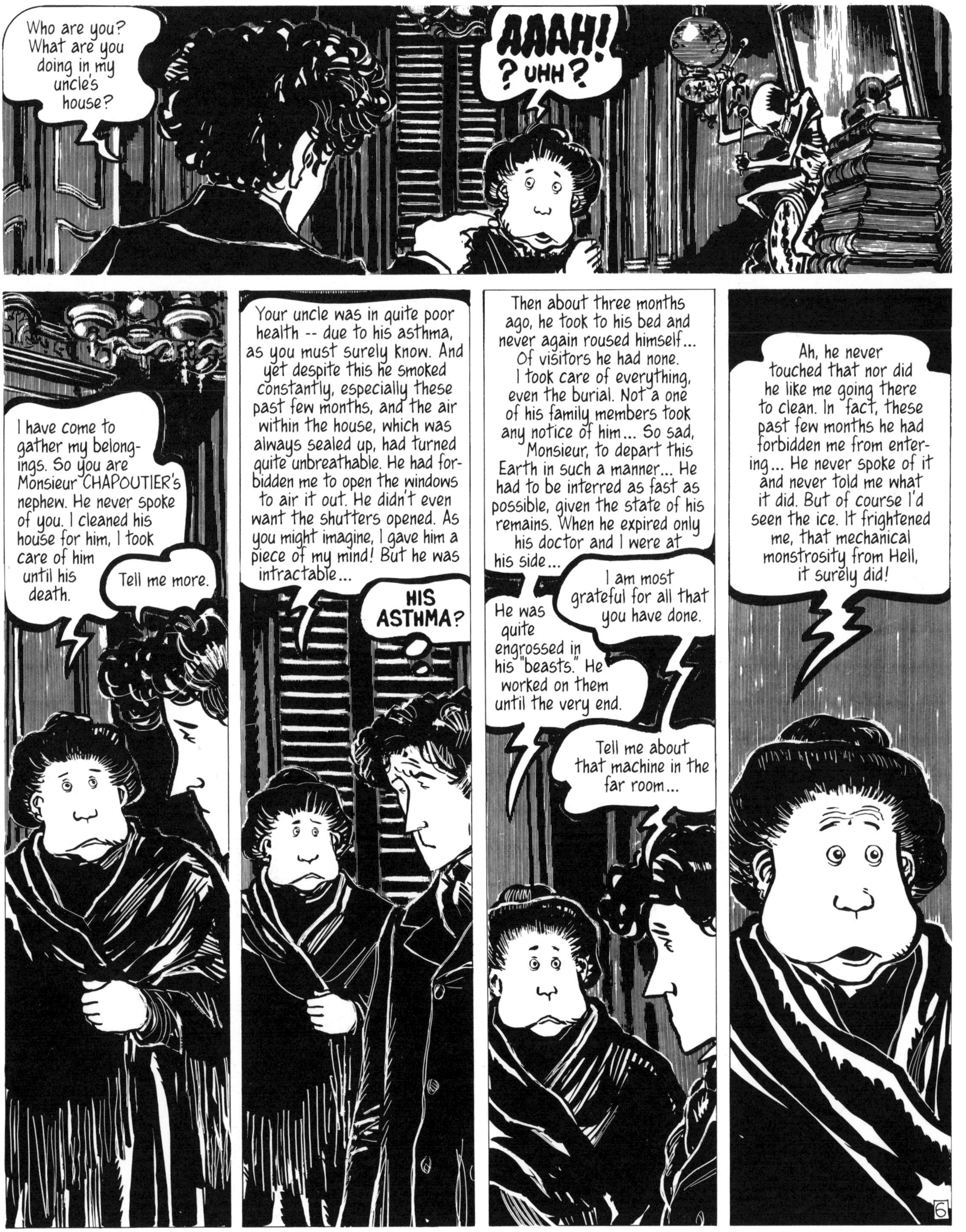
Who are you? What are you doing in my uncle's house?
AAAH! ? UHH ?
I have come to gather my belongings. So you are Monsieur CHAPOUTIER's nephew. He never spoke of you. I cleaned his house for him, I took care of him until his death.
Tell me more.
Your uncle was in quite poor health -- due to his asthma, as you must surely know. And yet despite this he smoked constantly, especially these past few months, and the air within the house, which was always sealed up, had turned quite unbreathable. He had forbidden me to open the windows to air it out. He didn't even want the shutters opened. As you might imagine, I gave him a piece of my mind! But he was intractable...
HIS ASTHMA?
Then about three months ago, he took to his bed and never again roused himself... Of visitors he had none. I took care of everything, even the burial. Not a one of his family members took any notice of him... So sad, Monsieur, to depart this Earth in such a manner... He had to be interred as fast as possible, given the state of his remains. When he expired only his doctor and I were at his side...
I am most grateful for all that you have done.
He was quite engrossed in his "beasts." He worked on them until the very end.
Tell me about that machine in the far room...
Ah, he never touched that nor did he like me going there to clean. In fact, these past few months he had forbidden me from entering... He never spoke of it and never told me what it did. But of course I'd seen the ice. It frightened me, that mechanical monstrosity from Hell, it surely did!
6

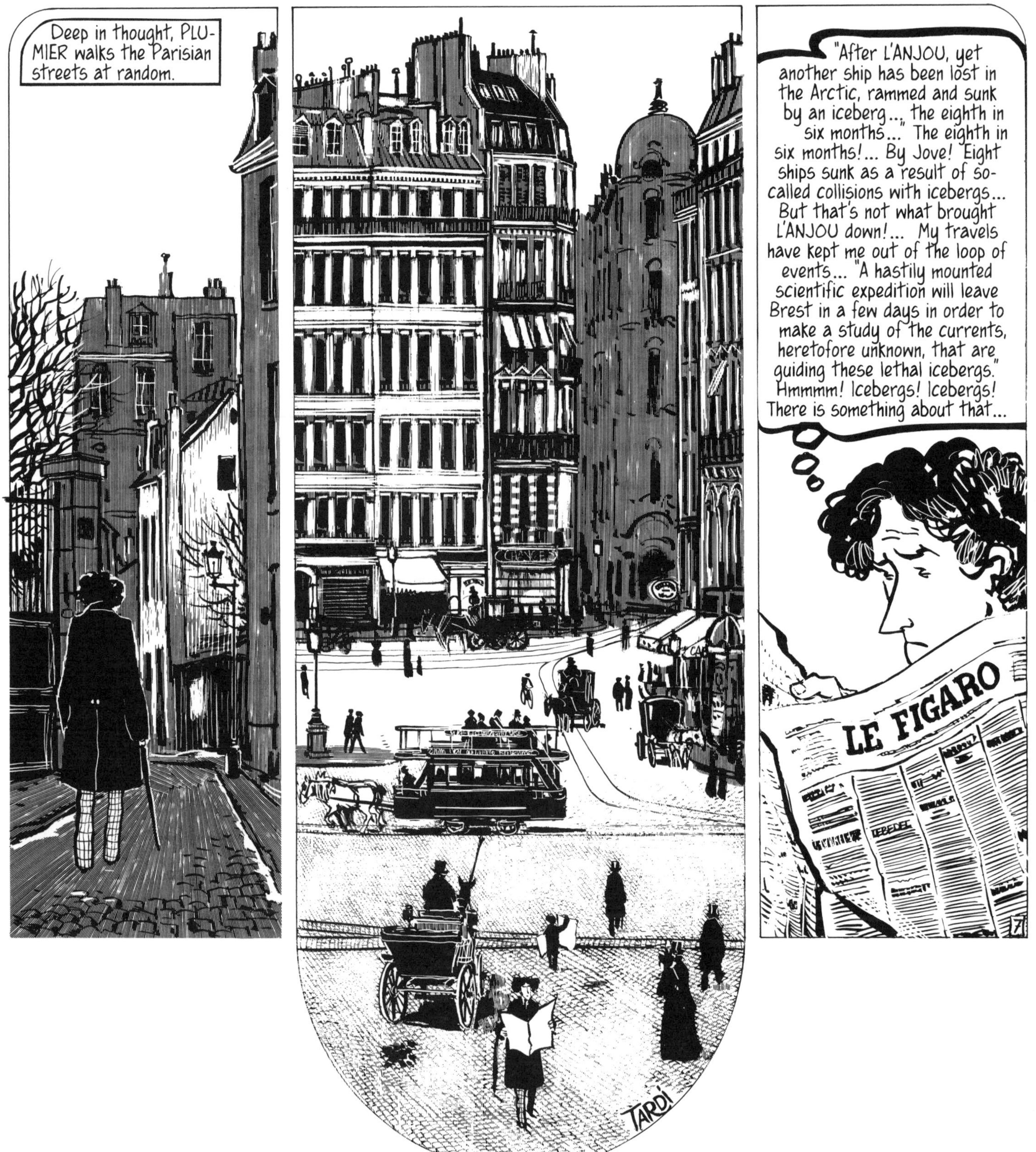
Deep in thought, PLUMIER walks the Parisian streets at random.
TARDI
"After L'ANJOU, yet another ship has been lost in the Arctic, rammed and sunk by an iceberg..., the eighth in six months..." The eighth in six months!... By Jove! Eight ships sunk as a result of so-called collisions with icebergs... But that's not what brought L'ANJOU down!... My travels have kept me out of the loop of events... "A hastily mounted scientific expedition will leave Brest in a few days in order to make a study of the currents, heretofore unknown, that are guiding these lethal icebergs." Hmmmm! Icebergs! Icebergs! There is something about that...
LE FIGARO

His heart full to bursting with a dull anxiety and his head aswirl with questions, J. PLUMIER wanders. He senses there to be something disturbing about CHAPOUTIER's death. His uncle did smoke, true, but it had come as news to him that his uncle suffered from asthma. And this obsession with locking himself up did not seem like the old tinkerer! Those animals glimpsed within the formaldehyde? CHAPOUTIER had never experimented upon living creatures! And, more than anything else, that extraordinary machine with its tubing covered in ice, apparently abandoned in great haste, as if during his Uncle's research the animal species has suddenly vaulted to greater importance than these enigmatic mechanical creations. And finally this news in the newspaper -- these tales of icebergs. But there was no link.. Yet J. PLUMIER's stride takes on a greater decisiveness. Has he divined the solution to all of these mysteries?

III

NIGHT TRAIN TO BREST

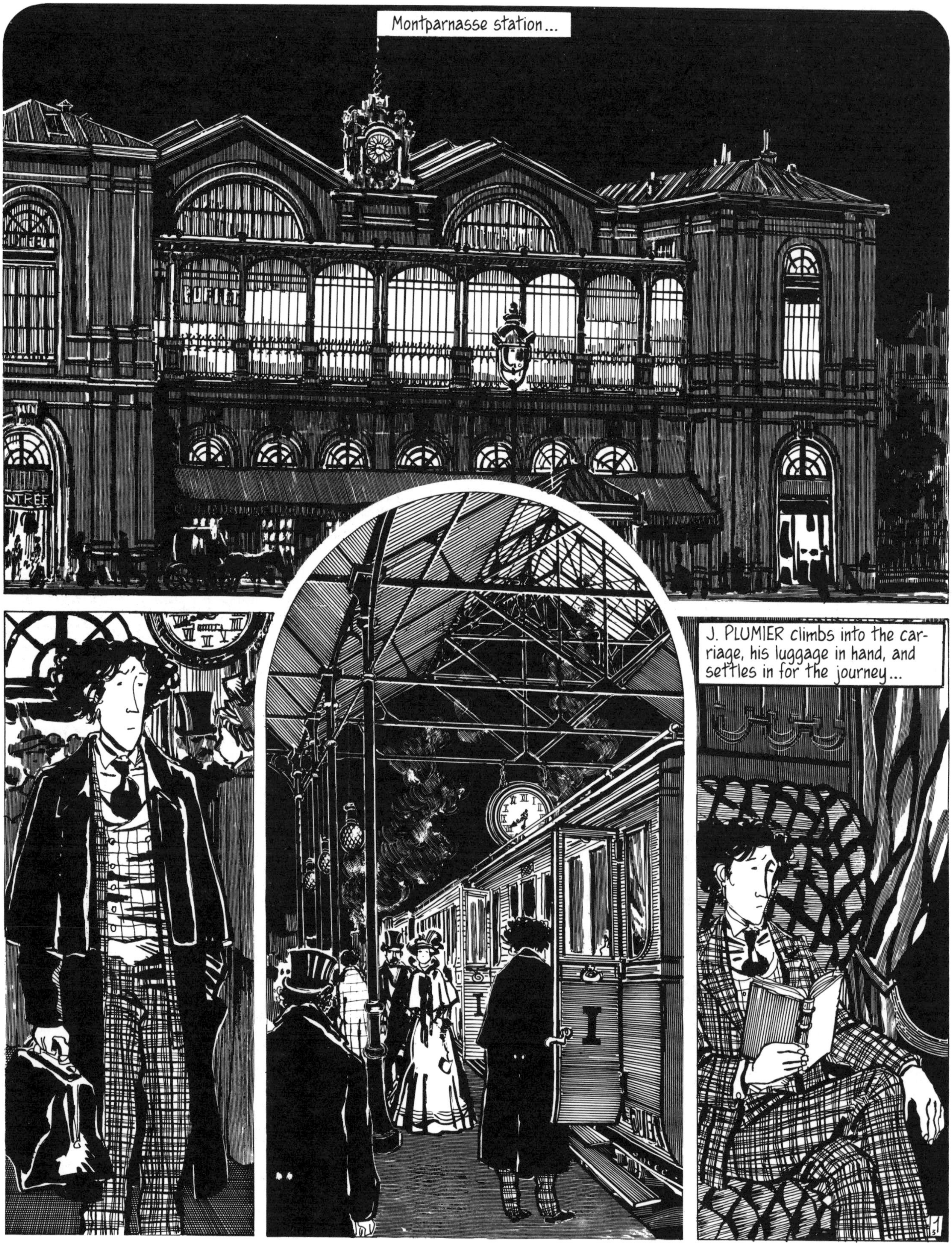
Montparnasse station...
J. PLUMIER climbs into the carriage, his luggage in hand, and settles in for the journey...

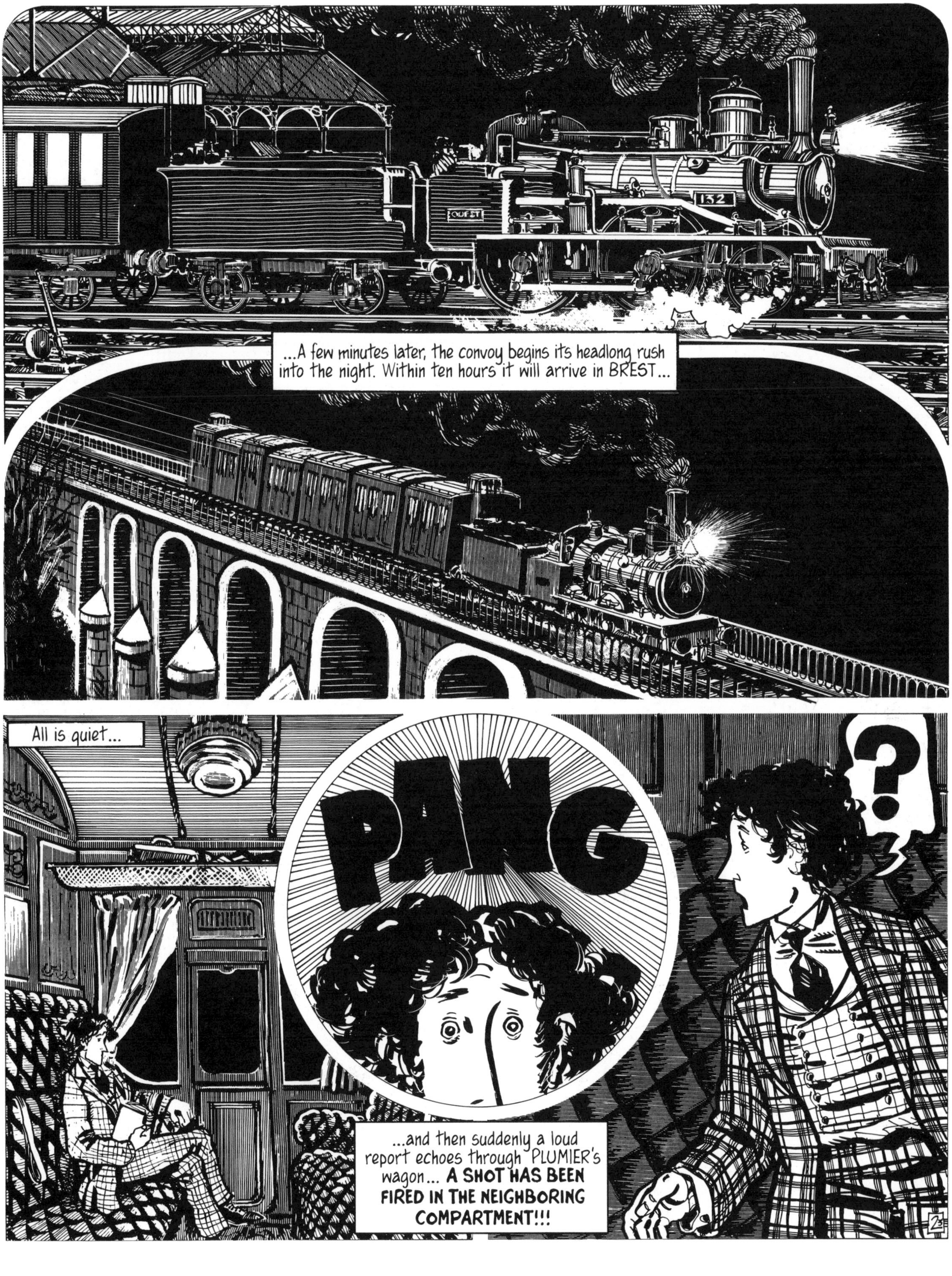
OUEST
132
...A few minutes later, the convoy begins its headlong rush into the night. Within ten hours it will arrive in BREST...
All is quiet...
PANG
?
...and then suddenly a loud report echoes through PLUMIER's wagon... A SHOT HAS BEEN FIRED IN THE NEIGHBORING COMPARTMENT!!!

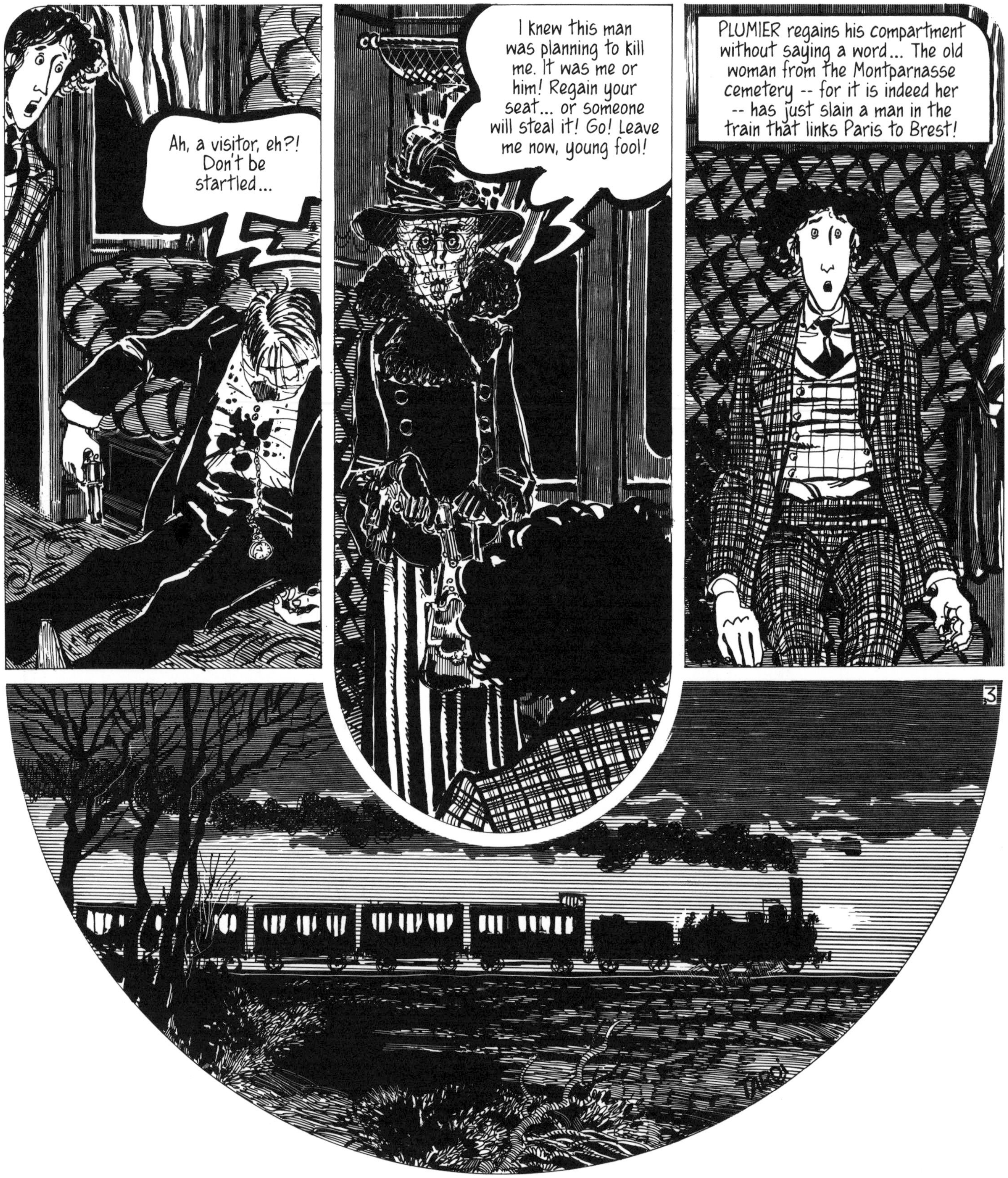
Ah, a visitor, eh?! Don't be startled...
I knew this man was planning to kill me. It was me or him! Regain your seat... or someone will steal it! Go! Leave me now, young fool!
PLUMIER regains his compartment without saying a word... The old woman from the Montparnasse cemetery -- for it is indeed her -- has just slain a man in the train that links Paris to Brest!
3

J. PLUMIER spends the rest of the trip as if nailed to his banquette, astonished beyond speech by this latest occurrence. Does this slaying have anything to do with the bizarre adventure, the exploration of whose mysterious halls he has begun and in which he is rapidly becoming lost? Does the appearance of this unknown woman -- glimpsed at the Montparnasse Cemetery lurking around L-F CHAPOUTIER's gravesite -- contribute in any way toward unraveling this strange story? J. PLUMIER would be stumped if enjoined to answer all these questions...

IV

FROM HIS SECRET ALLY

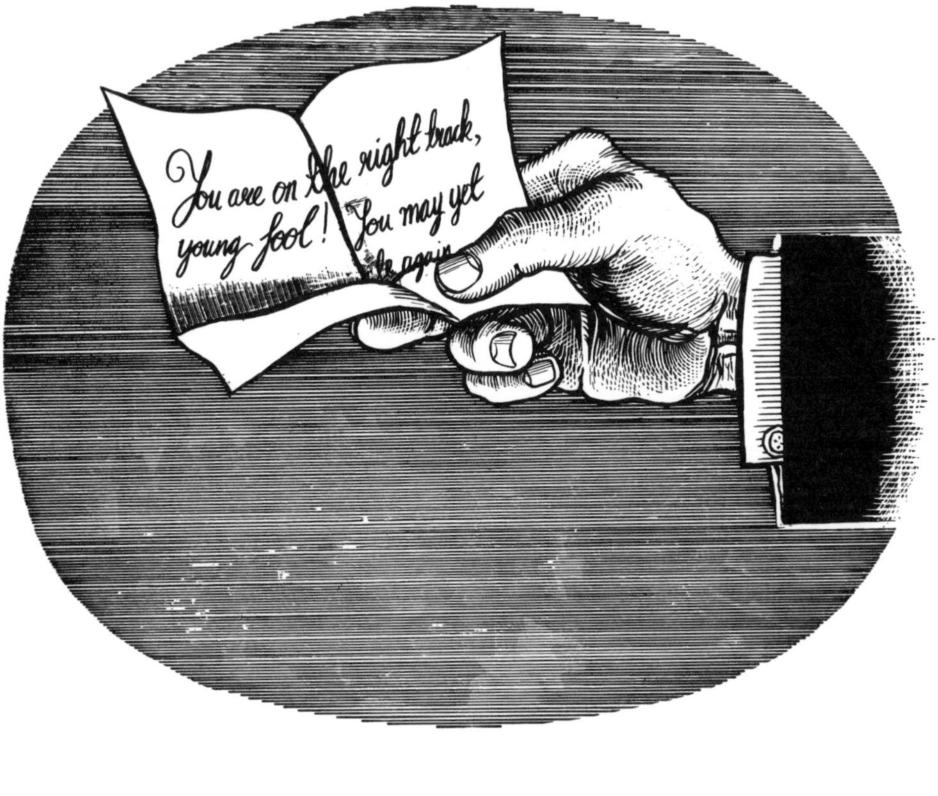
You are on the right track,
young fool! You may yet

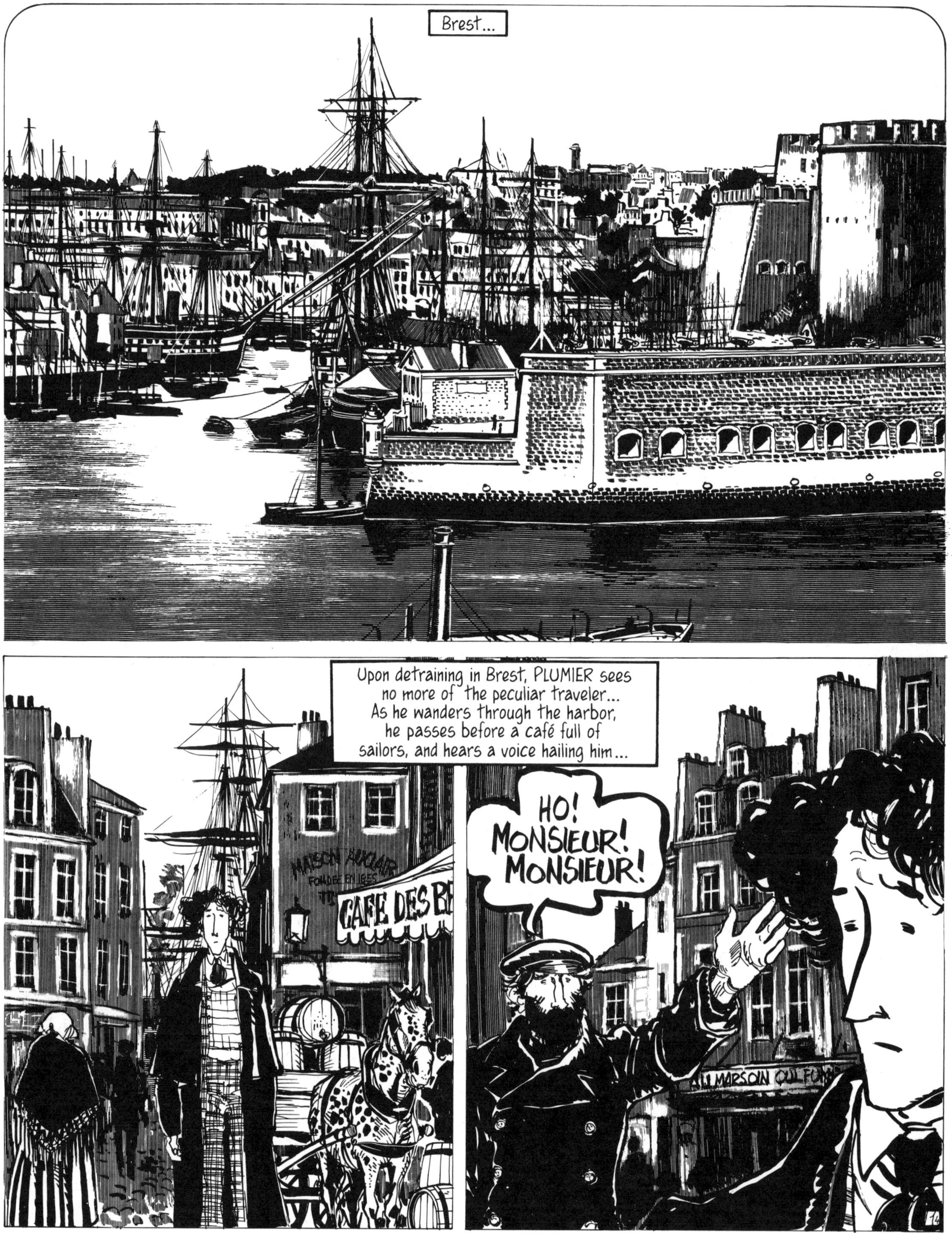
Brest...
Upon detraining in Brest, PLUMIER sees no more of the peculiar traveler... As he wanders through the harbor, he passes before a café full of sailors, and hears a voice hailing him...
HO! MONSIEUR! MONSIEUR!

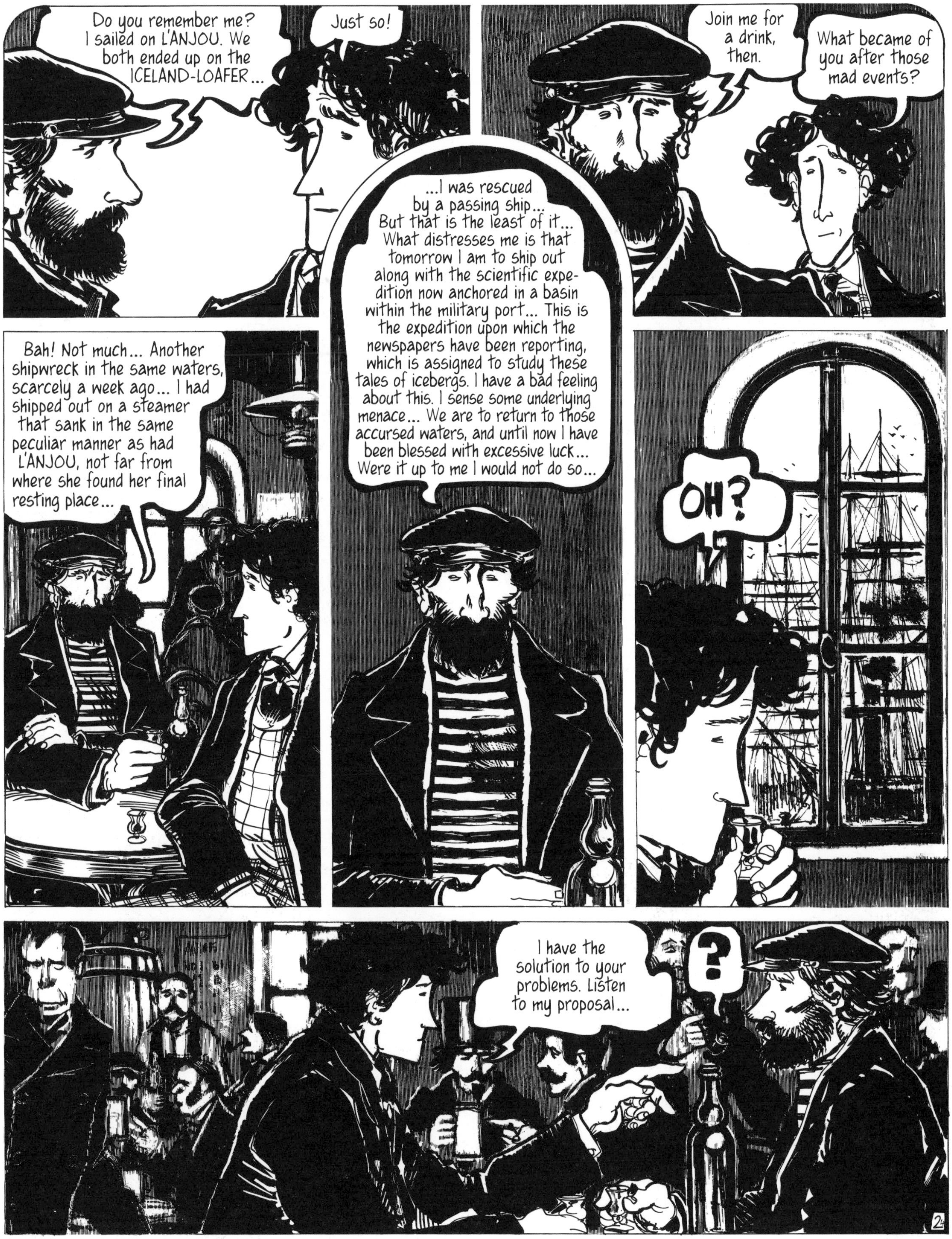

Do you remember me? I sailed on L'ANJOU. We both ended up on the ICELAND-LOAFER...
Just so!
Join me for a drink, then.
What became of you after those mad events?
Bah! Not much... Another shipwreck in the same waters, scarcely a week ago... I had shipped out on a steamer that sank in the same peculiar manner as had L'ANJOU, not far from where she found her final resting place...
...I was rescued by a passing ship... But that is the least of it... What distresses me is that tomorrow I am to ship out along with the scientific expedition now anchored in a basin within the military port... This is the expedition upon which the newspapers have been reporting, which is assigned to study these tales of icebergs. I have a bad feeling about this. I sense some underlying menace... We are to return to those accursed waters, and until now I have been blessed with excessive luck... Were it up to me I would not do so...
OH?
I have the solution to your problems. Listen to my proposal...
?

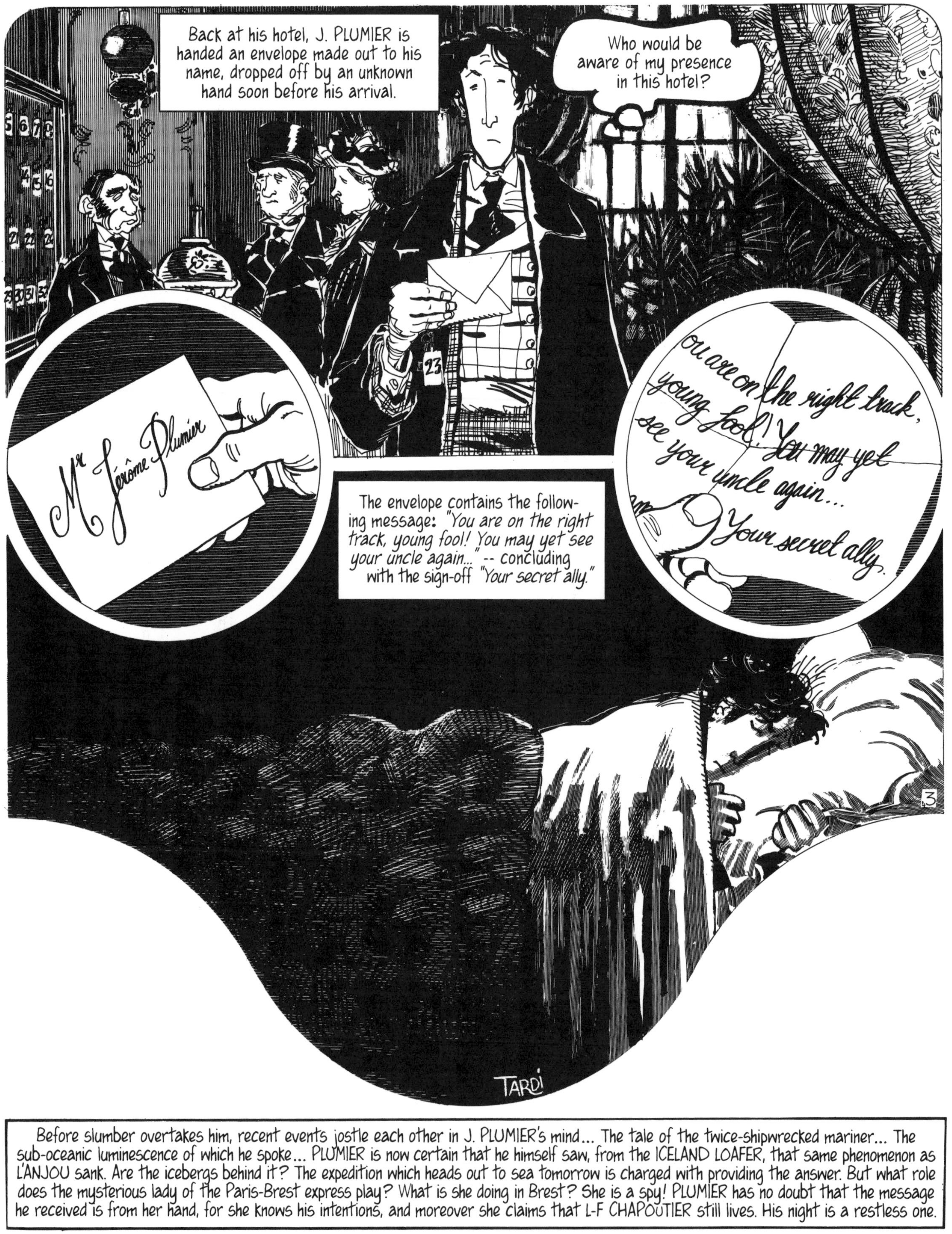
Back at his hotel, J. PLUMIER is handed an envelope made out to his name, dropped off by an unknown hand soon before his arrival.
Who would be aware of my presence in this hotel?
23
Mr Jérôme Plumier
The envelope contains the following message: "You are on the right track, young fool! You may yet see your uncle again..." -- concluding with the sign-off "Your secret ally."
ou are on the right track, young fool! You may yet see your uncle again...
Your secret ally.
3
TARDI

Before slumber overtakes him, recent events jostle each other in J. PLUMIER's mind... The tale of the twice-shipwrecked mariner... The sub-oceanic luminescence of which he spoke... PLUMIER is now certain that he himself saw, from the ICELAND LOAFER, that same phenomenon as L'ANJOU sank. Are the icebergs behind it? The expedition which heads out to sea tomorrow is charged with providing the answer. But what role does the mysterious lady of the Paris-Brest express play? What is she doing in Brest? She is a spy! PLUMIER has no doubt that the message he received is from her hand, for she knows his intentions, and moreover she claims that L-F CHAPOUTIER still lives. His night is a restless one.

V

AN ABRUPT END TO A FRENCH SCIENTIFIC EXPEDITION

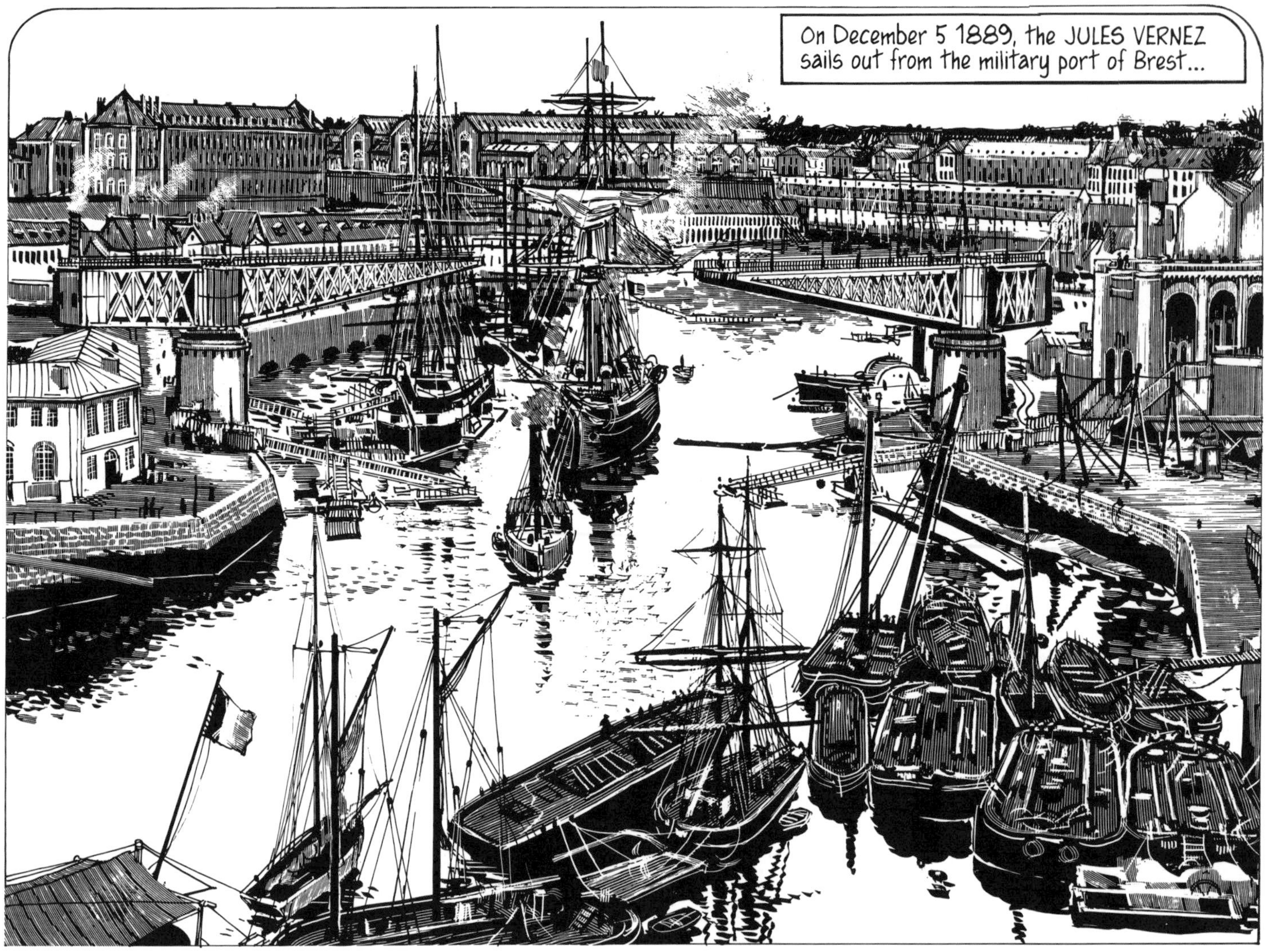
On December 5 1889, the JULES VERNEZ sails out from the military port of Brest...

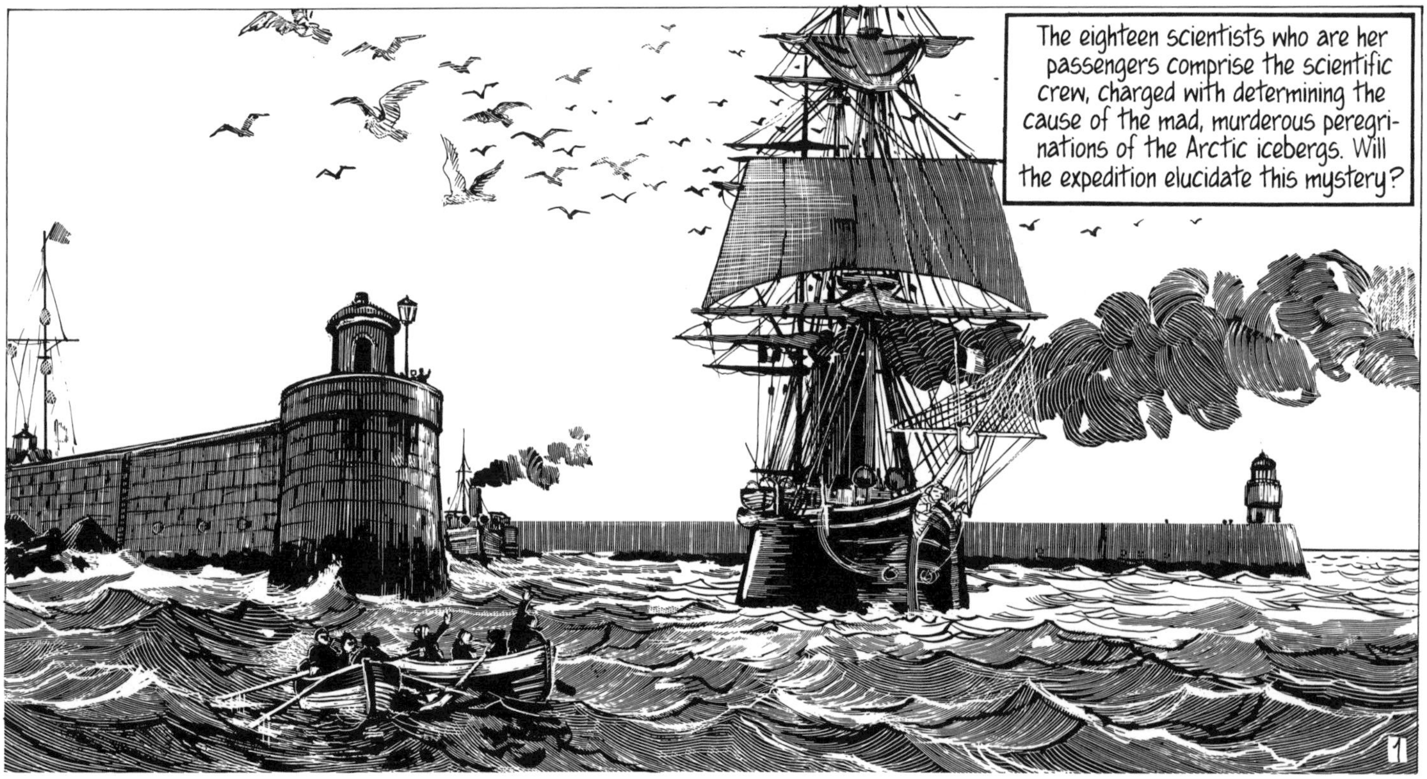
The eighteen scientists who are her passengers comprise the scientific crew, charged with determining the cause of the mad, murderous peregrinations of the Arctic icebergs. Will the expedition elucidate this mystery?

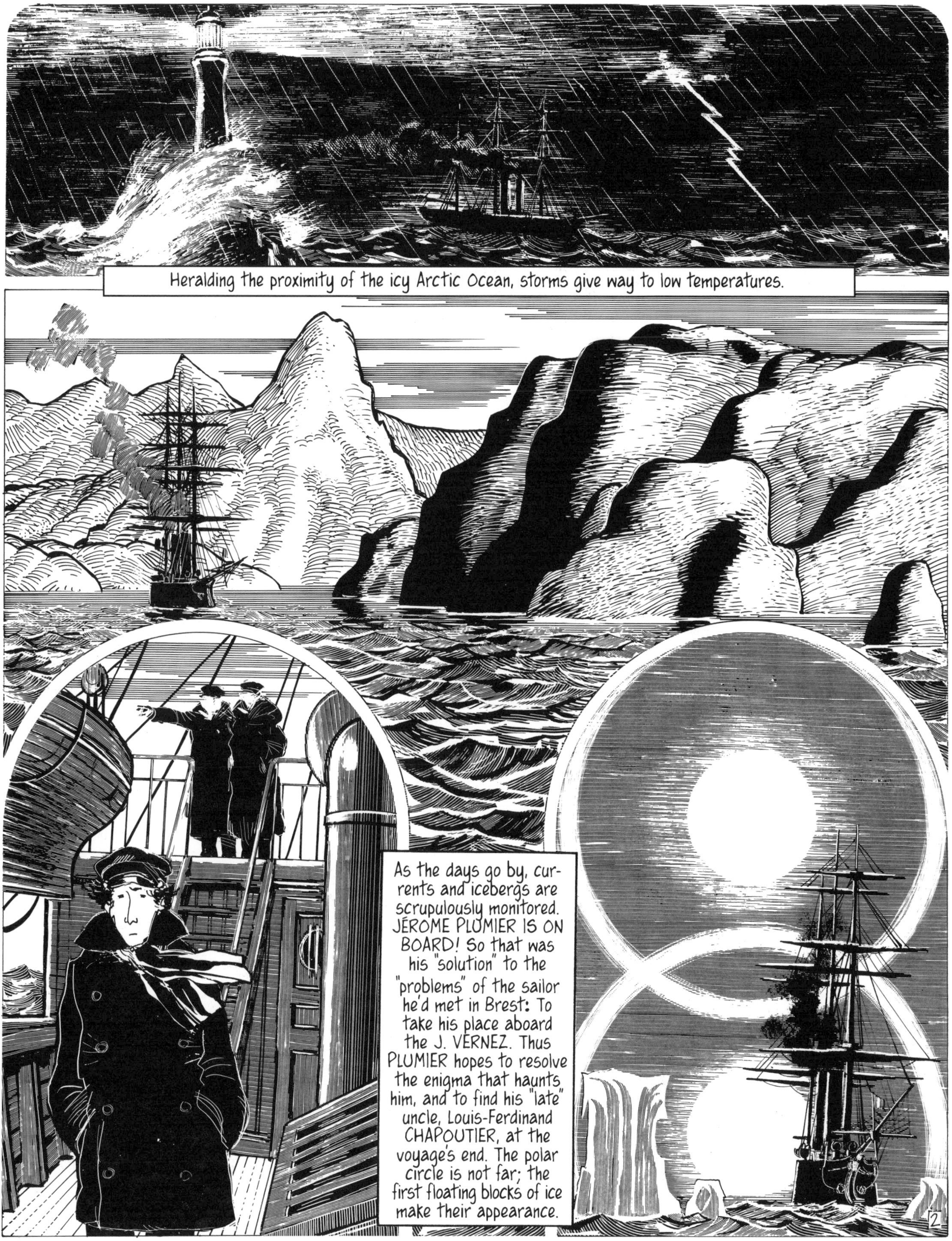
Heralding the proximity of the icy Arctic Ocean, storms give way to low temperatures.
As the days go by, currents and icebergs are scrupulously monitored. JÉROME PLUMIER IS ON BOARD! So that was his "solution" to the "problems" of the sailor he'd met in Brest: To take his place aboard the J. VERNEZ. Thus PLUMIER hopes to resolve the enigma that haunts him, and to find his "late" uncle, Louis-Ferdinand CHAPOUTIER, at the voyage's end. The polar circle is not far; the first floating blocks of ice make their appearance.
2

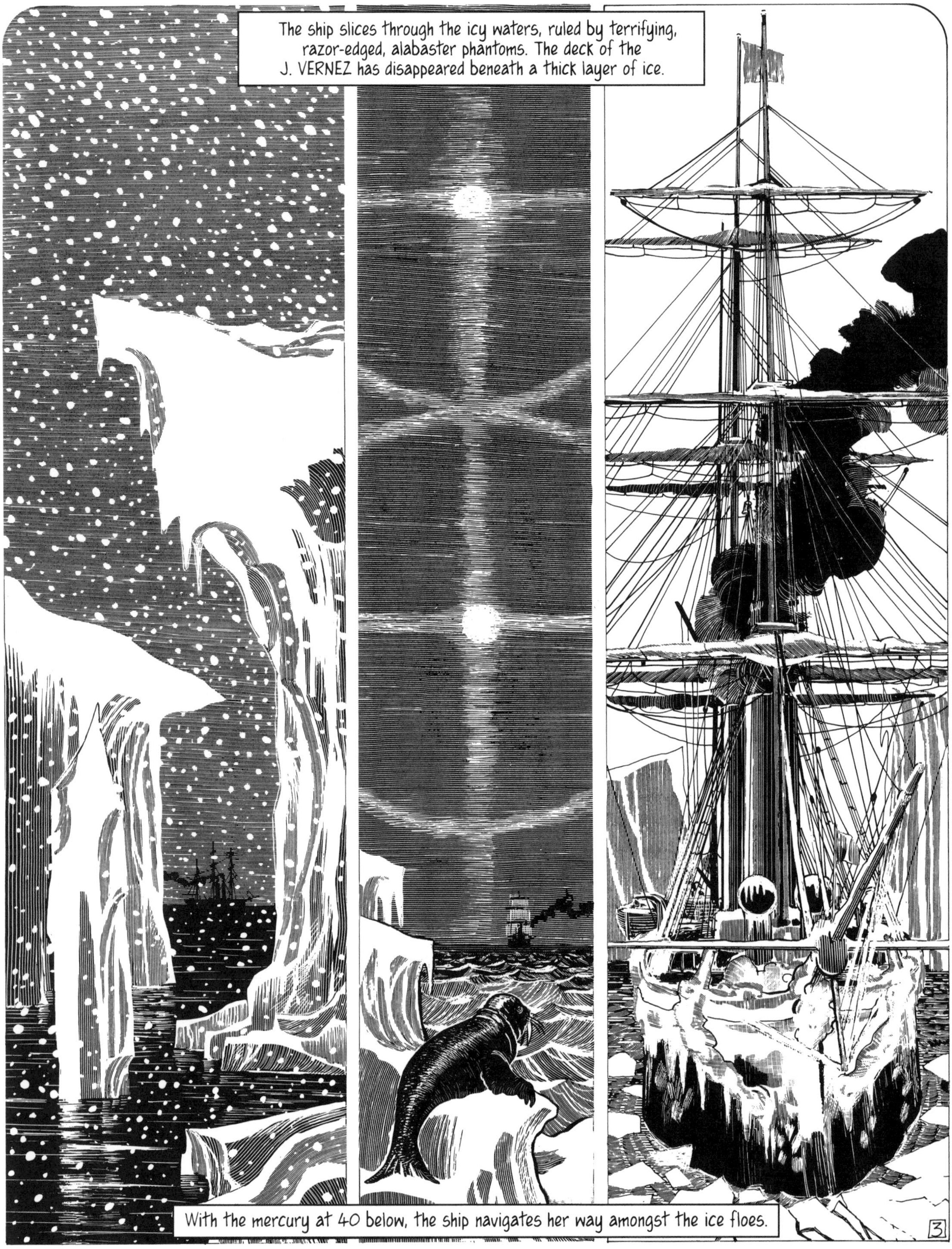
The ship slices through the icy waters, ruled by terrifying, razor-edged, alabaster phantoms. The deck of the J. VERNEZ has disappeared beneath a thick layer of ice.
With the mercury at 40 below, the ship navigates her way amongst the ice floes.
3

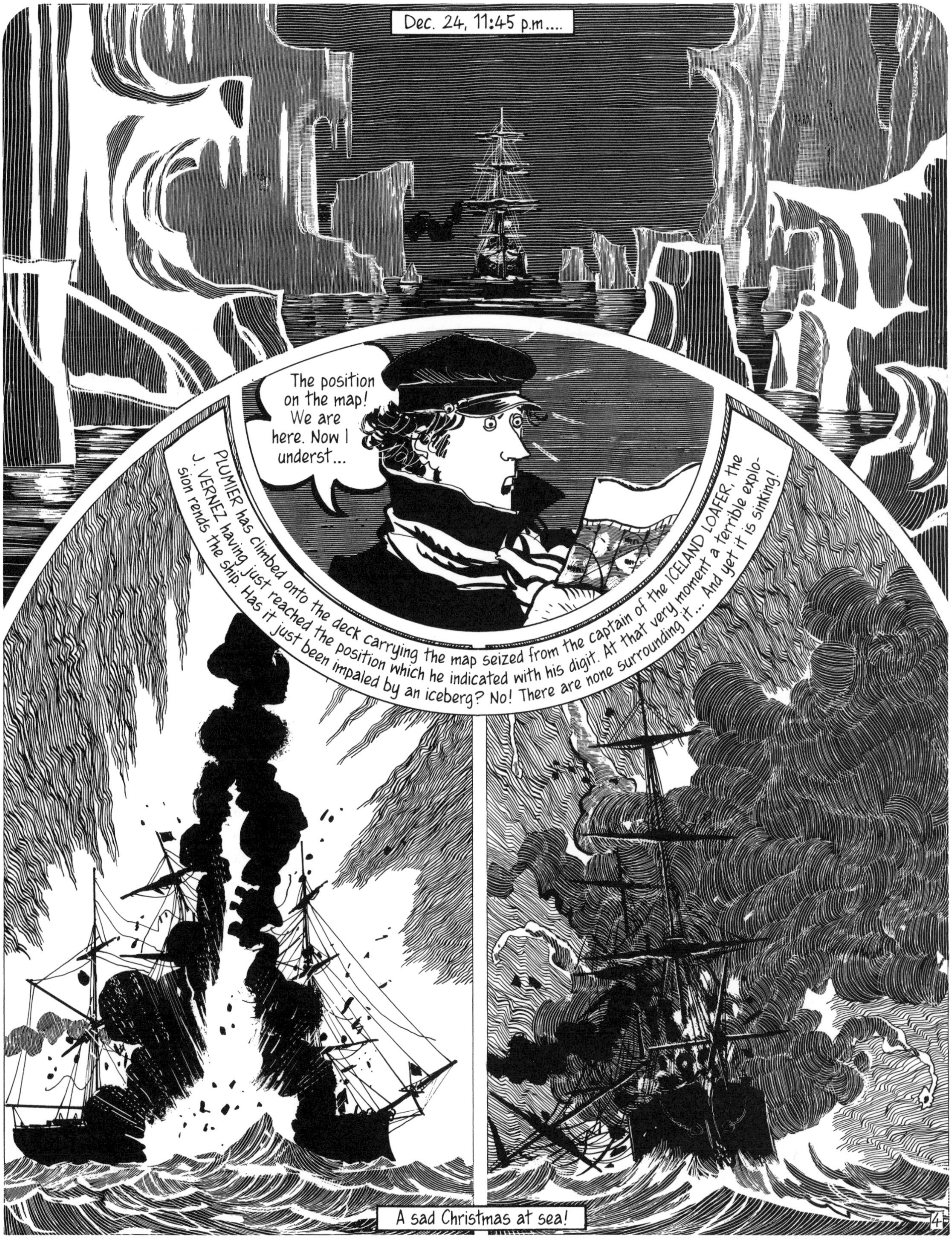

Dec. 24, 11:45 p.m....
The position on the map! We are here. Now I underst...
PLUMIER has climbed onto the deck carrying the map seized from the captain of the ICELAND LOAFER, the J. VERNEZ having just reached the position which he indicated with his digit. At that very moment a terrible explosion rends the ship. Has it just been impaled by an iceberg? No! There are none surrounding it... And yet it is sinking!
A sad Christmas at sea!
4

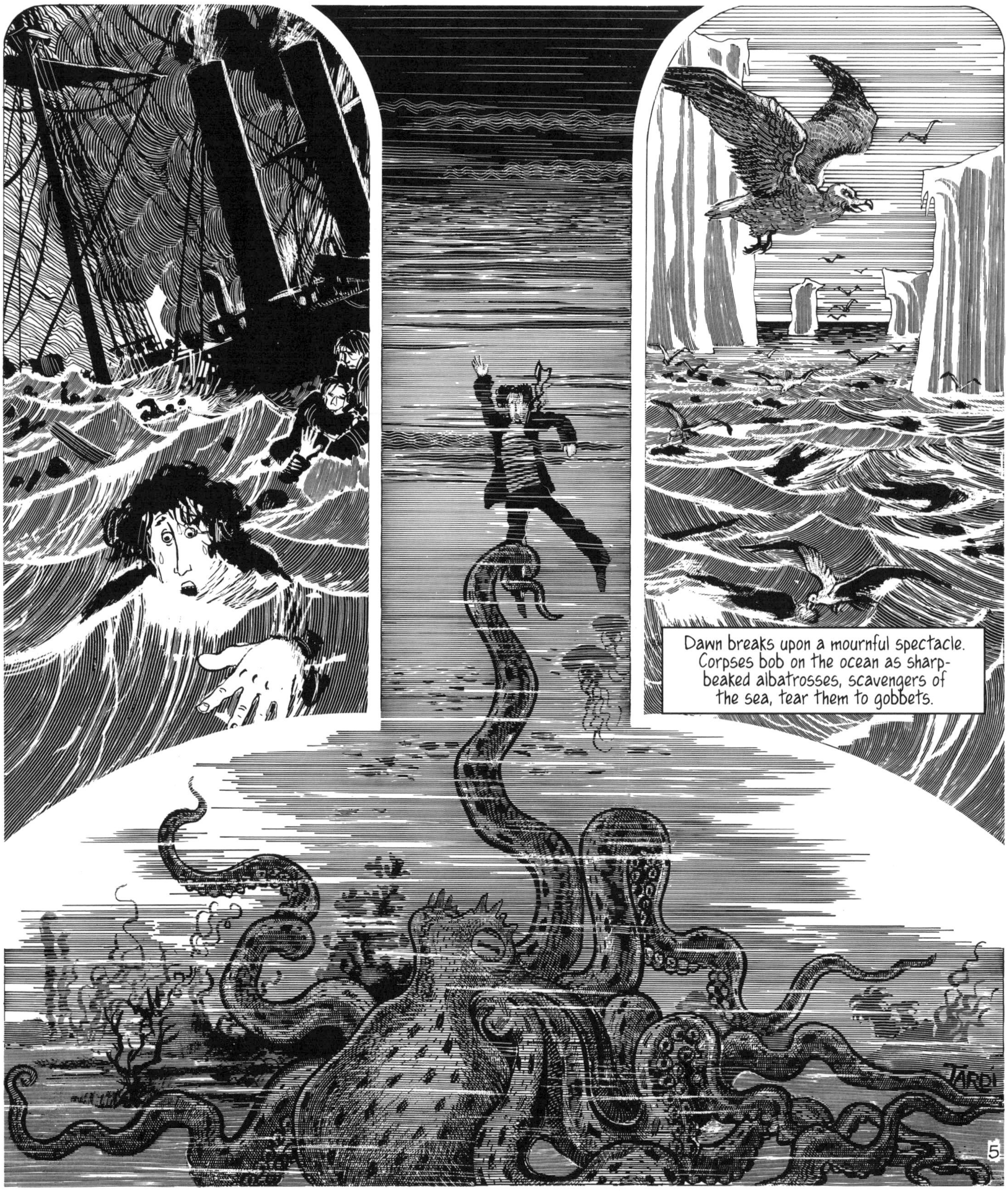
Dawn breaks upon a mournful spectacle. Corpses bob on the ocean as sharp-beaked albatrosses, scavengers of the sea, tear them to gobbets.
TARDI
5

The JULES VERNEZ sinks, pulling down its crew in its wake, putting an end to the French scientific expedition... Jérôme PLUMIER plummets into the ocean's icy depths, in the grip of a hideously tentacled sea monster. Might this nightmarish vision be the result of the delirium that has overcome him -- one final chaotic and hallucinatory vision -- before his plunge into final darkness? Or perhaps he is already dead? As the J. VERNEZ reached the mysterious position indicated by the captain of the ICELAND LOAFER, PLUMIER appeared to grasp some truth... but which one?

VI

IN THE BELLY OF THE BEAST

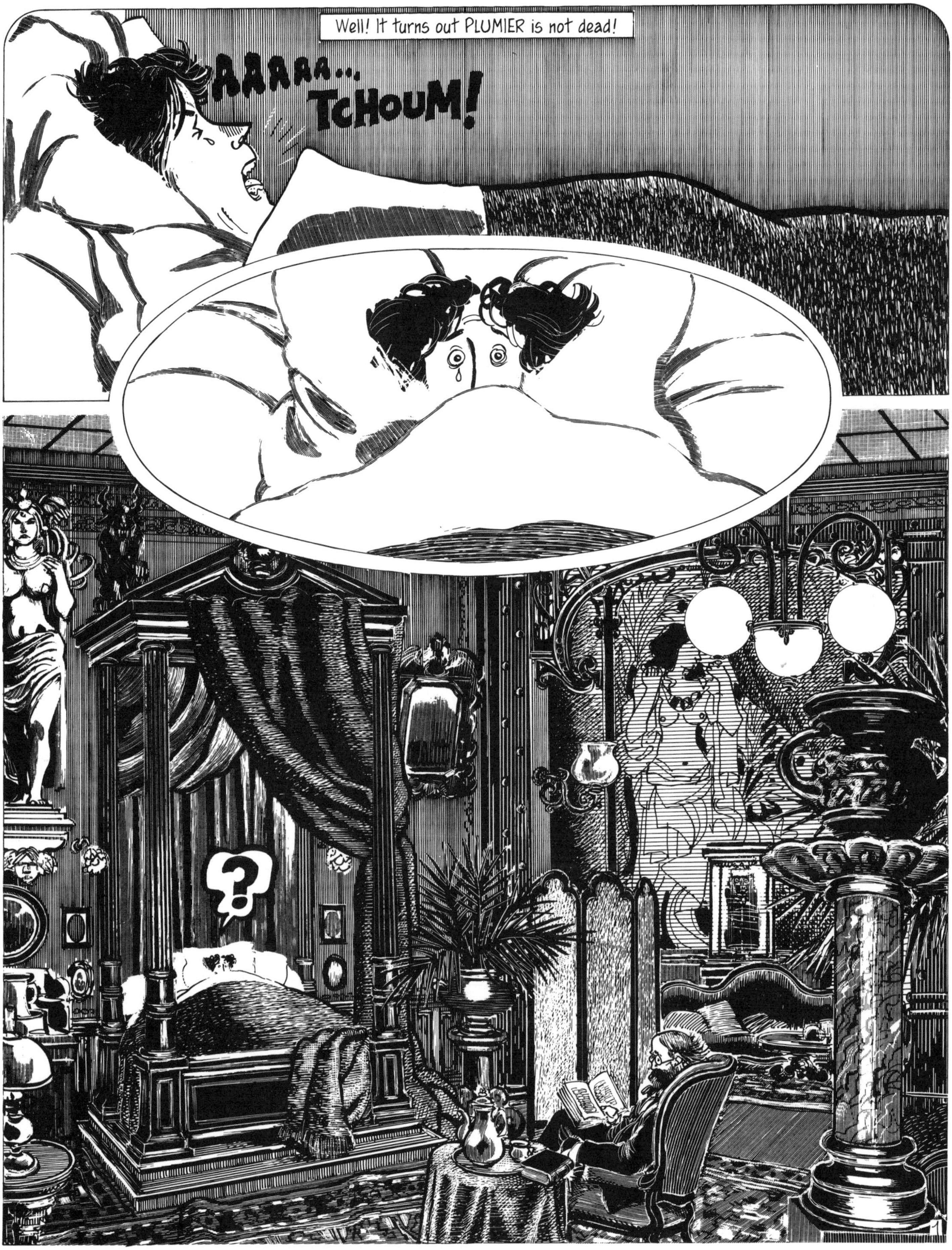
Well! It turns out PLUMIER is not dead!
AAAAA... TCHOUM!
?

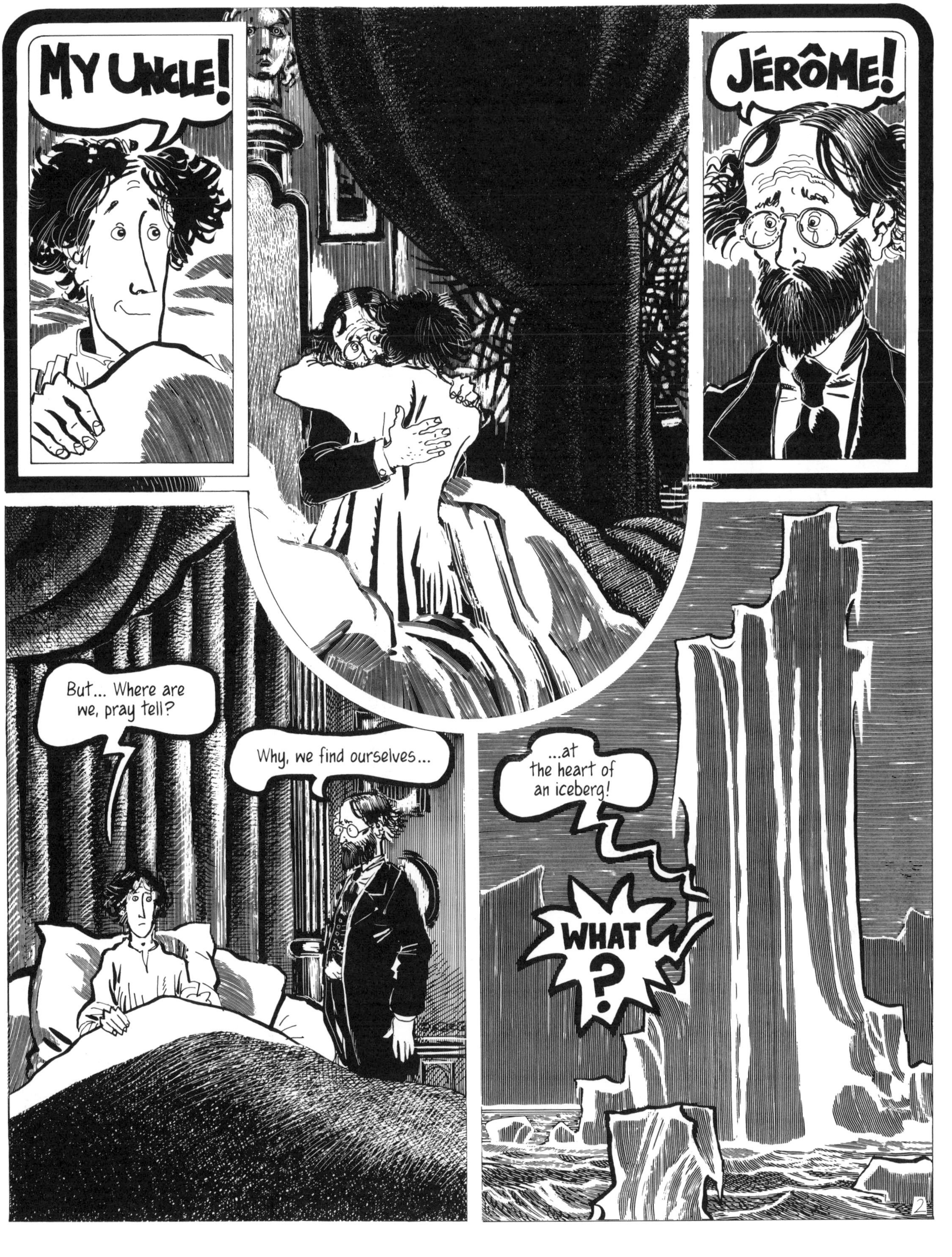
MY UNCLE!
JÉRÔME!
But... Where are we, pray tell?
Why, we find ourselves...
...at the heart of an iceberg!
WHAT ?
2

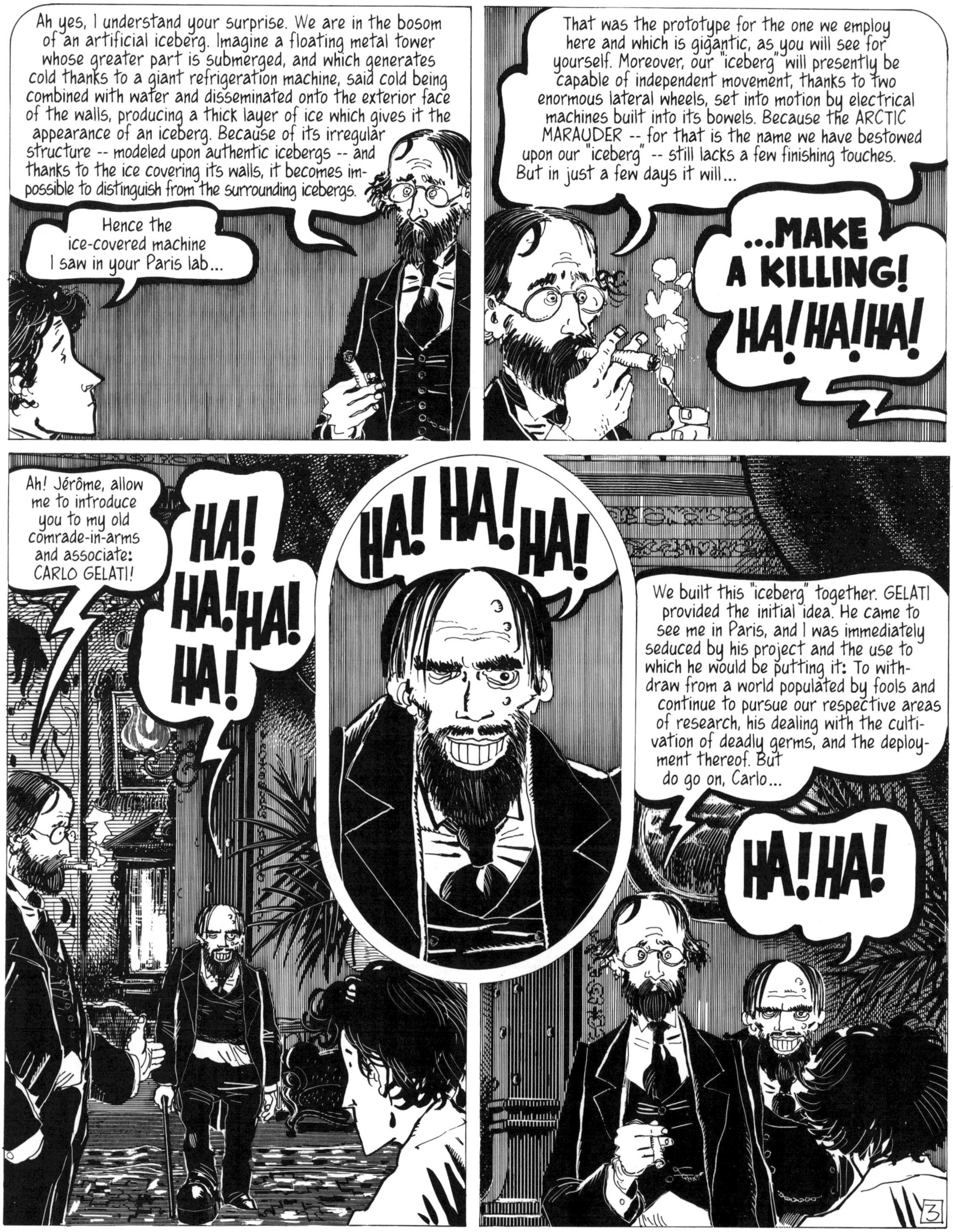

Ah yes, I understand your surprise. We are in the bosom of an artificial iceberg. Imagine a floating metal tower whose greater part is submerged, and which generates cold thanks to a giant refrigeration machine, said cold being combined with water and disseminated onto the exterior face of the walls, producing a thick layer of ice which gives it the appearance of an iceberg. Because of its irregular structure -- modeled upon authentic icebergs -- and thanks to the ice covering its walls, it becomes impossible to distinguish from the surrounding icebergs.
Hence the ice-covered machine I saw in your Paris lab...
That was the prototype for the one we employ here and which is gigantic, as you will see for yourself. Moreover, our "iceberg" will presently be capable of independent movement, thanks to two enormous lateral wheels, set into motion by electrical machines built into its bowels. Because the ARCTIC MARAUDER -- for that is the name we have bestowed upon our "iceberg" -- still lacks a few finishing touches. But in just a few days it will...
...MAKE A KILLING! HA! HA! HA!
Ah! Jérôme, allow me to introduce you to my old comrade-in-arms and associate: CARLO GELATI!
HA! HA! HA! HA!
HA! HA! HA!
We built this "iceberg" together. GELATI provided the initial idea. He came to see me in Paris, and I was immediately seduced by his project and the use to which he would be putting it: To withdraw from a world populated by fools and continue to pursue our respective areas of research, his dealing with the cultivation of deadly germs, and the deployment thereof. But do go on, Carlo...
HA! HA!
3

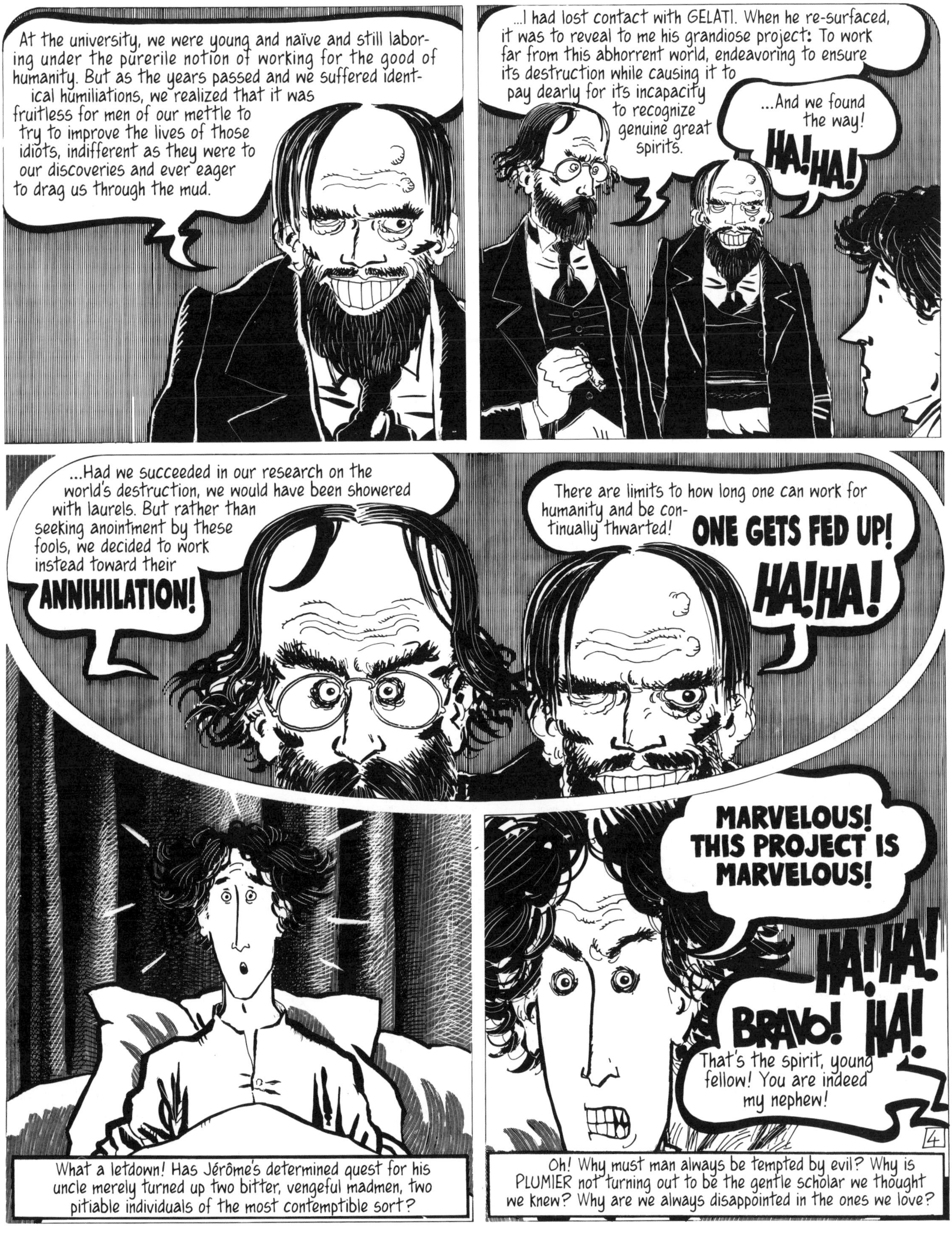
At the university, we were young and naïve and still laboring under the purerile notion of working for the good of humanity. But as the years passed and we suffered identical humiliations, we realized that it was fruitless for men of our mettle to try to improve the lives of those idiots, indifferent as they were to our discoveries and ever eager to drag us through the mud.
...I had lost contact with GELATI. When he re-surfaced, it was to reveal to me his grandiose project: To work far from this abhorrent world, endeavoring to ensure its destruction while causing it to pay dearly for its incapacity to recognize genuine great spirits.
...And we found the way! HA! HA!
...Had we succeeded in our research on the world's destruction, we would have been showered with laurels. But rather than seeking anointment by these fools, we decided to work instead toward their ANNIHILATION!
There are limits to how long one can work for humanity and be continually thwarted! ONE GETS FED UP! HA! HA!
MARVELOUS! THIS PROJECT IS MARVELOUS!
HA! HA! HA!
BRAVO! That's the spirit, young fellow! You are indeed my nephew!
4
What a letdown! Has Jérôme's determined quest for his uncle merely turned up two bitter, vengeful madmen, two pitiable individuals of the most contemptible sort?
Oh! Why must man always be tempted by evil? Why is PLUMIER not turning out to be the gentle scholar we thought we knew? Why are we always disappointed in the ones we love?

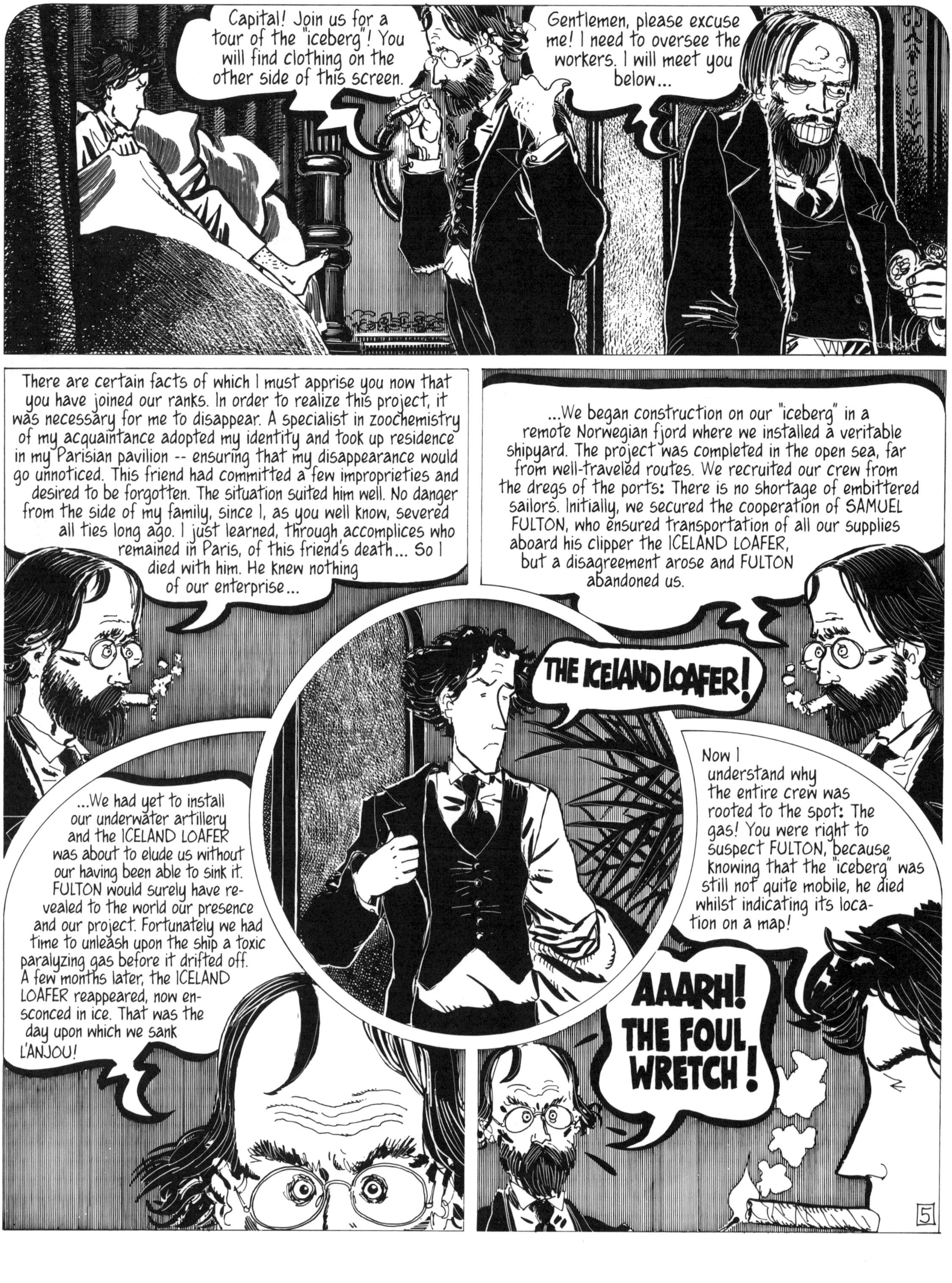
Capital! Join us for a tour of the "iceberg"! You will find clothing on the other side of this screen.
Gentlemen, please excuse me! I need to oversee the workers. I will meet you below...
There are certain facts of which I must apprise you now that you have joined our ranks. In order to realize this project, it was necessary for me to disappear. A specialist in zoochemistry of my acquaintance adopted my identity and took up residence in my Parisian pavilion -- ensuring that my disappearance would go unnoticed. This friend had committed a few improprieties and desired to be forgotten. The situation suited him well. No danger from the side of my family, since I, as you well know, severed all ties long ago. I just learned, through accomplices who remained in Paris, of this friend's death... So I died with him. He knew nothing of our enterprise...
...We began construction on our "iceberg" in a remote Norwegian fjord where we installed a veritable shipyard. The project was completed in the open sea, far from well-traveled routes. We recruited our crew from the dregs of the ports: There is no shortage of embittered sailors. Initially, we secured the cooperation of SAMUEL FULTON, who ensured transportation of all our supplies aboard his clipper the ICELAND LOAFER, but a disagreement arose and FULTON abandoned us.
THE ICELAND LOAFER!
...We had yet to install our underwater artillery and the ICELAND LOAFER was about to elude us without our having been able to sink it. FULTON would surely have revealed to the world our presence and our project. Fortunately we had time to unleash upon the ship a toxic paralyzing gas before it drifted off. A few months later, the ICELAND LOAFER reappeared, now ensconced in ice. That was the day upon which we sank L'ANJOU!
Now I understand why the entire crew was rooted to the spot: The gas! You were right to suspect FULTON, because knowing that the "iceberg" was still not quite mobile, he died whilst indicating its location on a map!
AAARH! THE FOUL WRETCH!
5

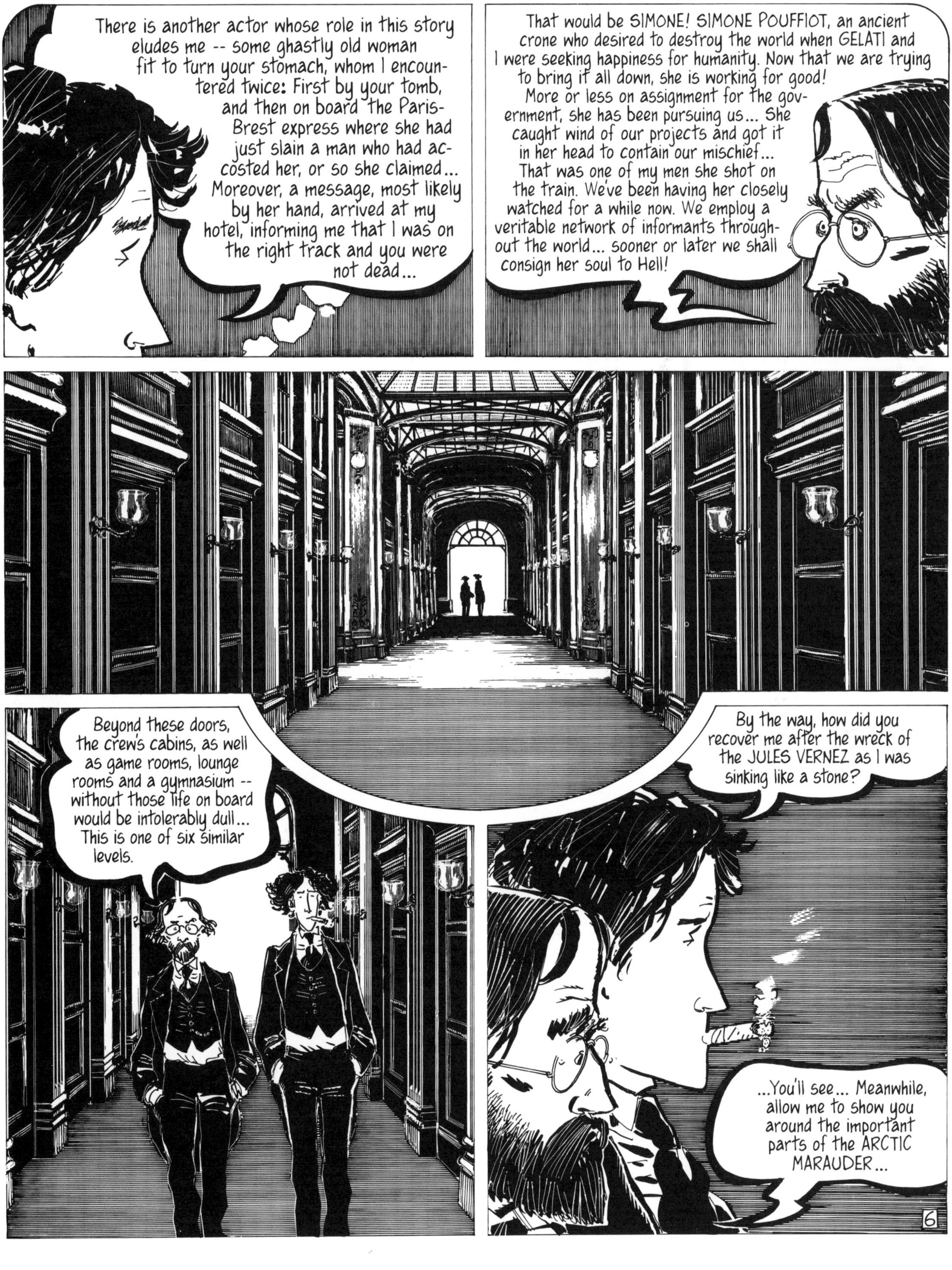
There is another actor whose role in this story eludes me -- some ghastly old woman fit to turn your stomach, whom I encountered twice: First by your tomb, and then on board the Paris-Brest express where she had just slain a man who had accosted her, or so she claimed... Moreover, a message, most likely by her hand, arrived at my hotel, informing me that I was on the right track and you were not dead...
That would be SIMONE! SIMONE POUFFIOT, an ancient crone who desired to destroy the world when GELATI and I were seeking happiness for humanity. Now that we are trying to bring it all down, she is working for good! More or less on assignment for the government, she has been pursuing us... She caught wind of our projects and got it in her head to contain our mischief... That was one of my men she shot on the train. We've been having her closely watched for a while now. We employ a veritable network of informants throughout the world... sooner or later we shall consign her soul to Hell!
Beyond these doors, the crew's cabins, as well as game rooms, lounge rooms and a gymnasium -- without those life on board would be intolerably dull... This is one of six similar levels.
By the way, how did you recover me after the wreck of the JULES VERNEZ as I was sinking like a stone?
...You'll see... Meanwhile, allow me to show you around the important parts of the ARCTIC MARAUDER...
6

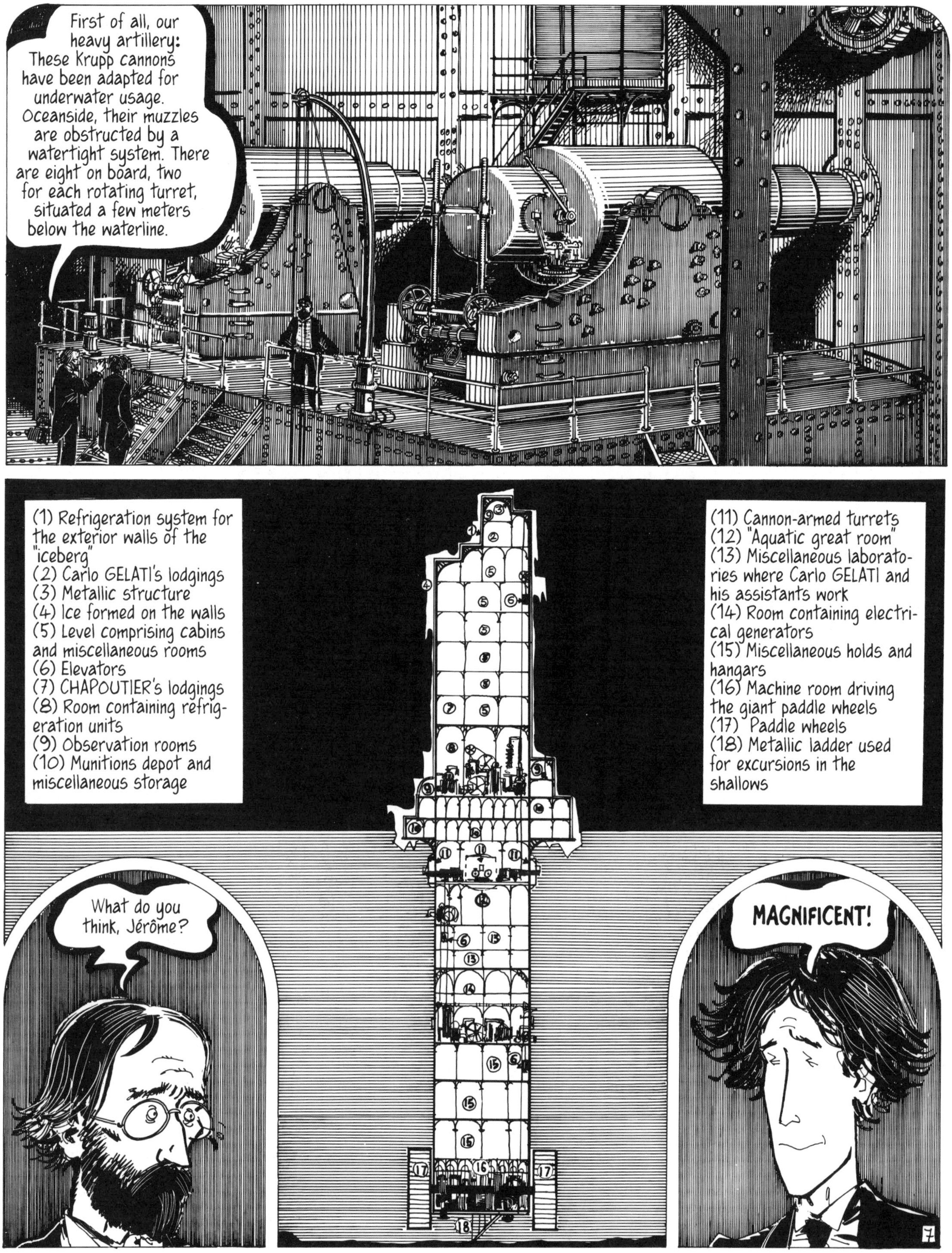
First of all, our heavy artillery: These Krupp cannons have been adapted for underwater usage. Oceanside, their muzzles are obstructed by a watertight system. There are eight on board, two for each rotating turret, situated a few meters below the waterline.
(1) Refrigeration system for the exterior walls of the "iceberg"
(2) Carlo GELATI's lodgings
(3) Metallic structure
(4) Ice formed on the walls
(5) Level comprising cabins and miscellaneous rooms
(6) Elevators
(7) CHAPOUTIER's lodgings
(8) Room containing refrigeration units
(9) Observation rooms
(10) Munitions depot and miscellaneous storage
(11) Cannon-armed turrets
(12) "Aquatic great room"
(13) Miscellaneous laboratories where Carlo GELATI and his assistants work
(14) Room containing electrical generators
(15) Miscellaneous holds and hangars
(16) Machine room driving the giant paddle wheels
(17) Paddle wheels
(18) Metallic ladder used for excursions in the shallows
What do you think, Jérôme?
MAGNIFICENT!

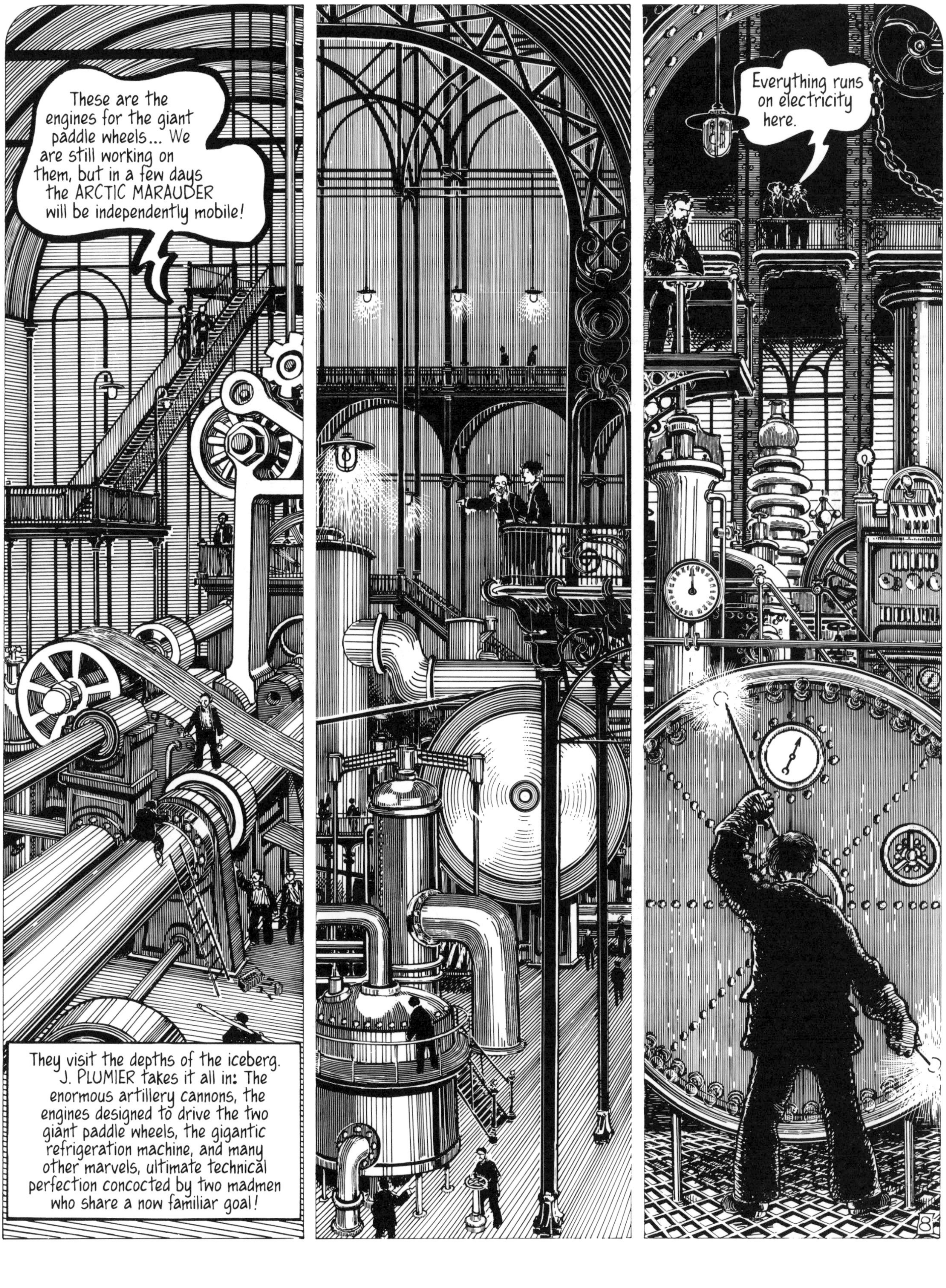
These are the engines for the giant paddle wheels... We are still working on them, but in a few days the ARCTIC MARAUDER will be independently mobile!
They visit the depths of the iceberg. J. PLUMIER takes it all in: The enormous artillery cannons, the engines designed to drive the two giant paddle wheels, the gigantic refrigeration machine, and many other marvels, ultimate technical perfection concocted by two madmen who share a now familiar goal!
Everything runs on electricity here.

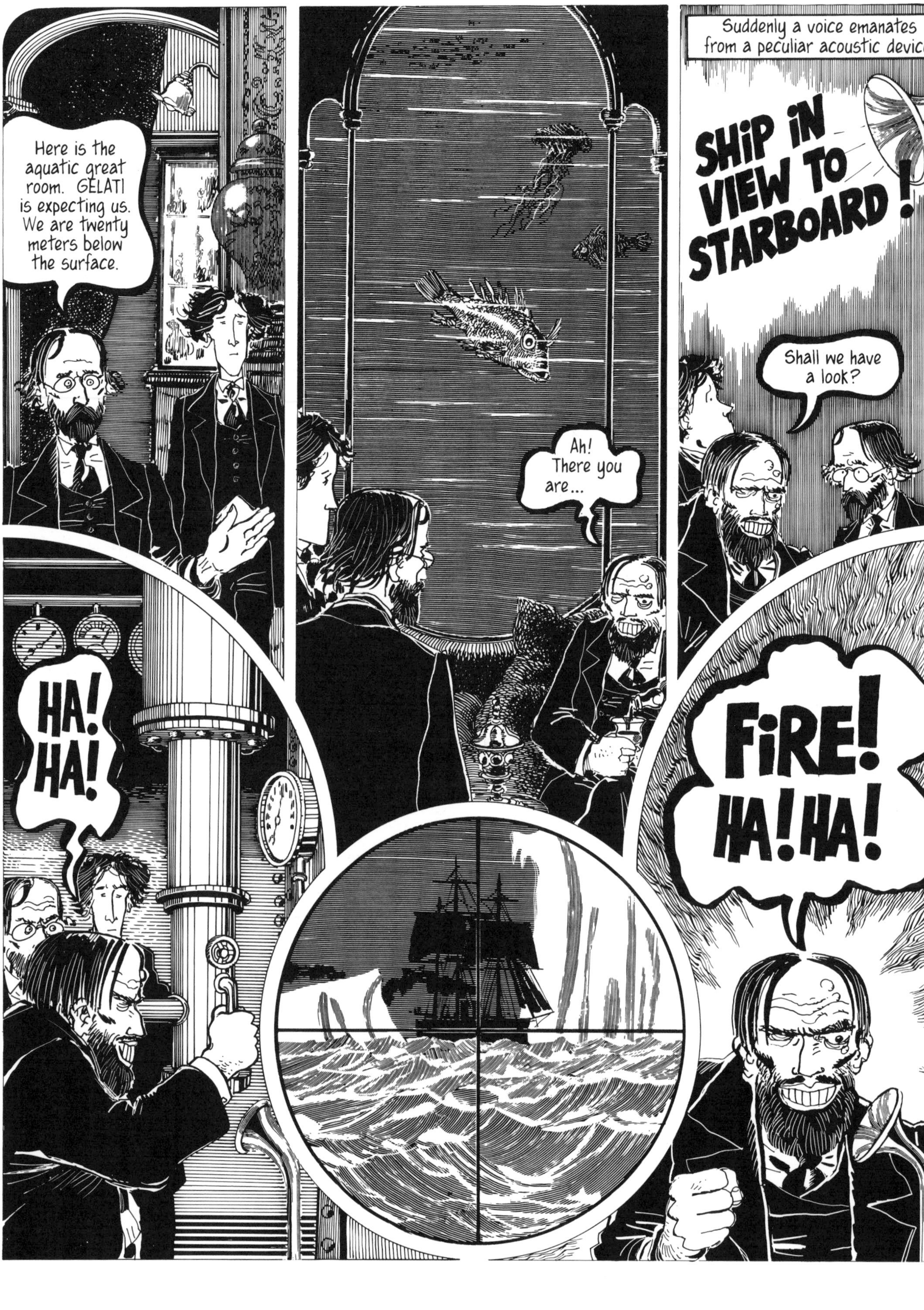

Here is the aquatic great room. GELATI is expecting us. We are twenty meters below the surface.
Ah! There you are...
Suddenly a voice emanates from a peculiar acoustic device.
SHIP IN VIEW TO STARBOARD!
Shall we have a look?
HA! HA!
FIRE! HA! HA!
9

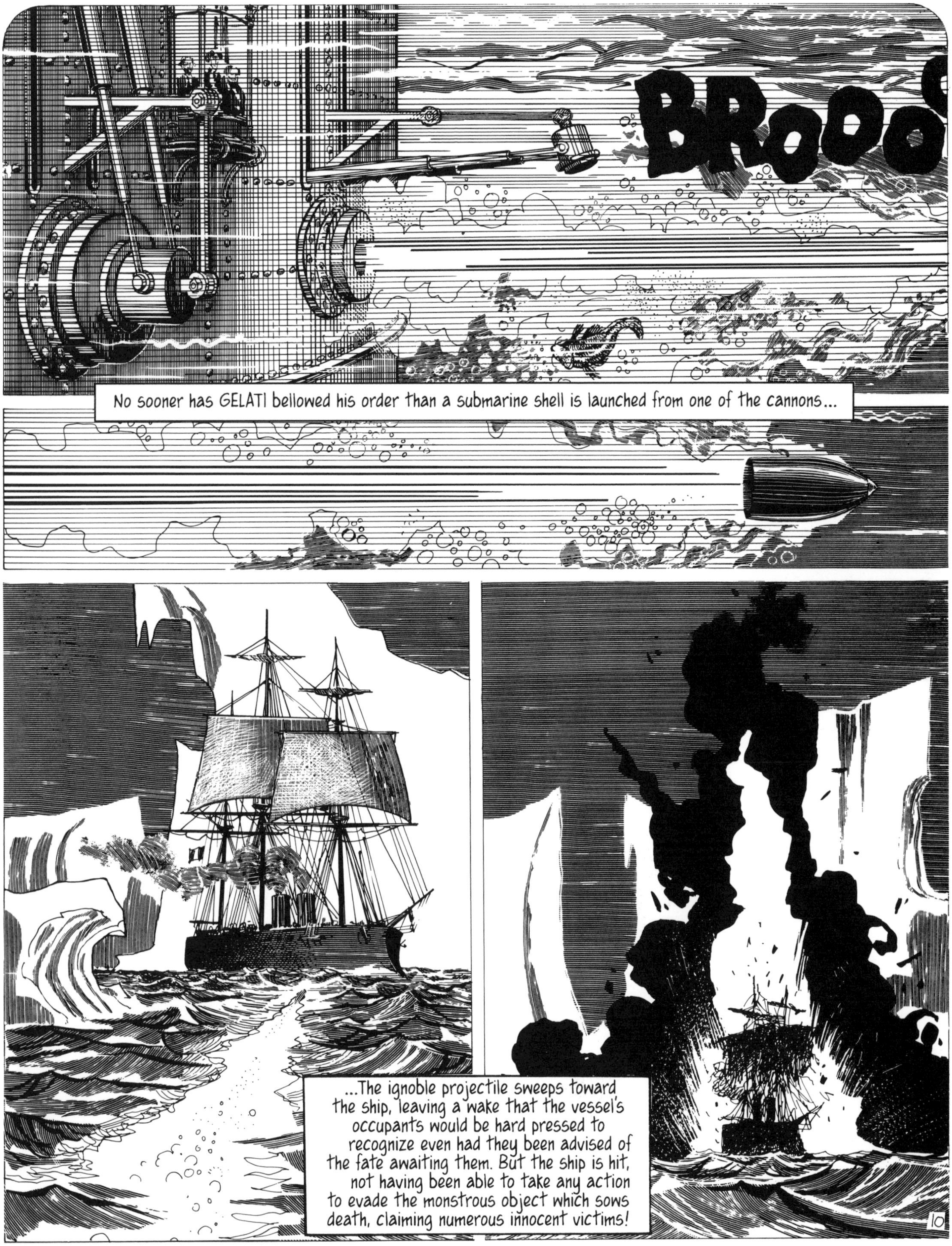
BROOO
No sooner has GELATI bellowed his order than a submarine shell is launched from one of the cannons...
...The ignoble projectile sweeps toward the ship, leaving a wake that the vessel's occupants would be hard pressed to recognize even had they been advised of the fate awaiting them. But the ship is hit, not having been able to take any action to evade the monstrous object which sows death, claiming numerous innocent victims!
10

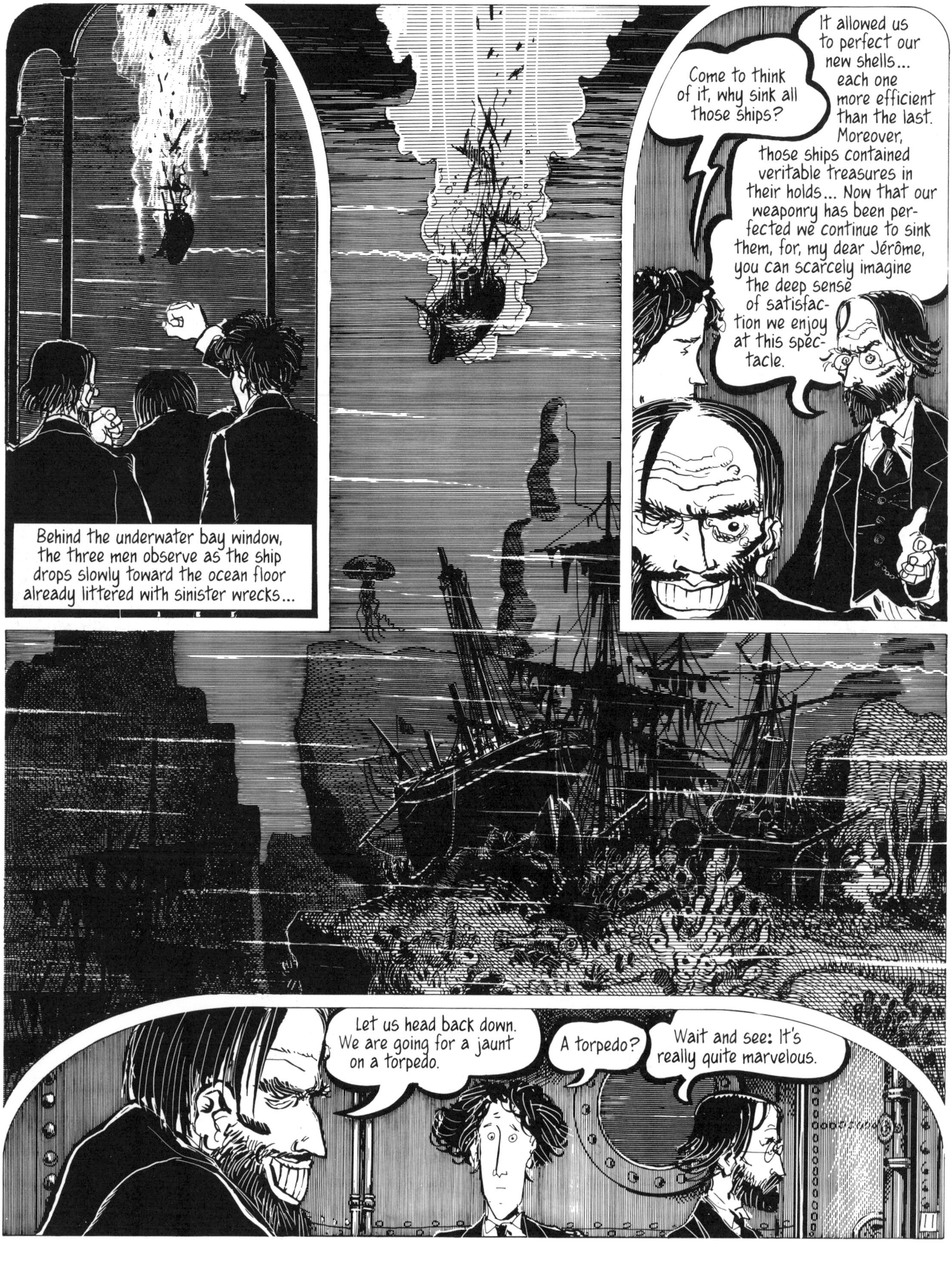
Behind the underwater bay window, the three men observe as the ship drops slowly toward the ocean floor already littered with sinister wrecks...
Come to think of it, why sink all those ships?
It allowed us to perfect our new shells... each one more efficient than the last. Moreover, those ships contained veritable treasures in their holds... Now that our weaponry has been perfected we continue to sink them, for, my dear Jérôme, you can scarcely imagine the deep sense of satisfaction we enjoy at this spectacle.
Let us head back down. We are going for a jaunt on a torpedo.
A torpedo?
Wait and see: It's really quite marvelous.

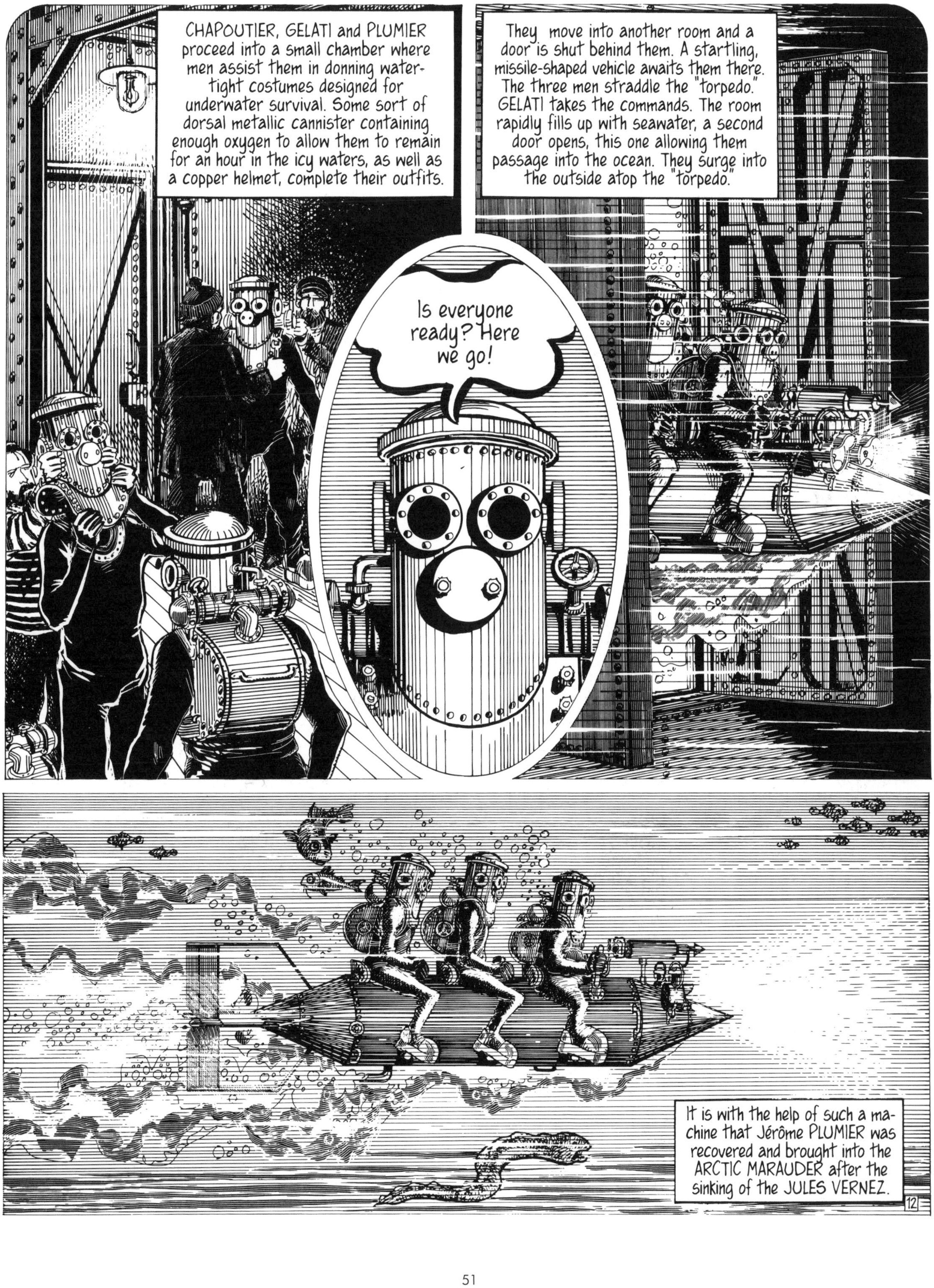
CHAPOUTIER, GELATI and PLUMIER proceed into a small chamber where men assist them in donning water-tight costumes designed for underwater survival. Some sort of dorsal metallic cannister containing enough oxygen to allow them to remain for an hour in the icy waters, as well as a copper helmet, complete their outfits.
They move into another room and a door is shut behind them. A startling, missile-shaped vehicle awaits them there. The three men straddle the "torpedo." GELATI takes the commands. The room rapidly fills up with seawater, a second door opens, this one allowing them passage into the ocean. They surge into the outside atop the "torpedo."
Is everyone ready? Here we go!
It is with the help of such a machine that Jérôme PLUMIER was recovered and brought into the ARCTIC MARAUDER after the sinking of the JULES VERNEZ.
12

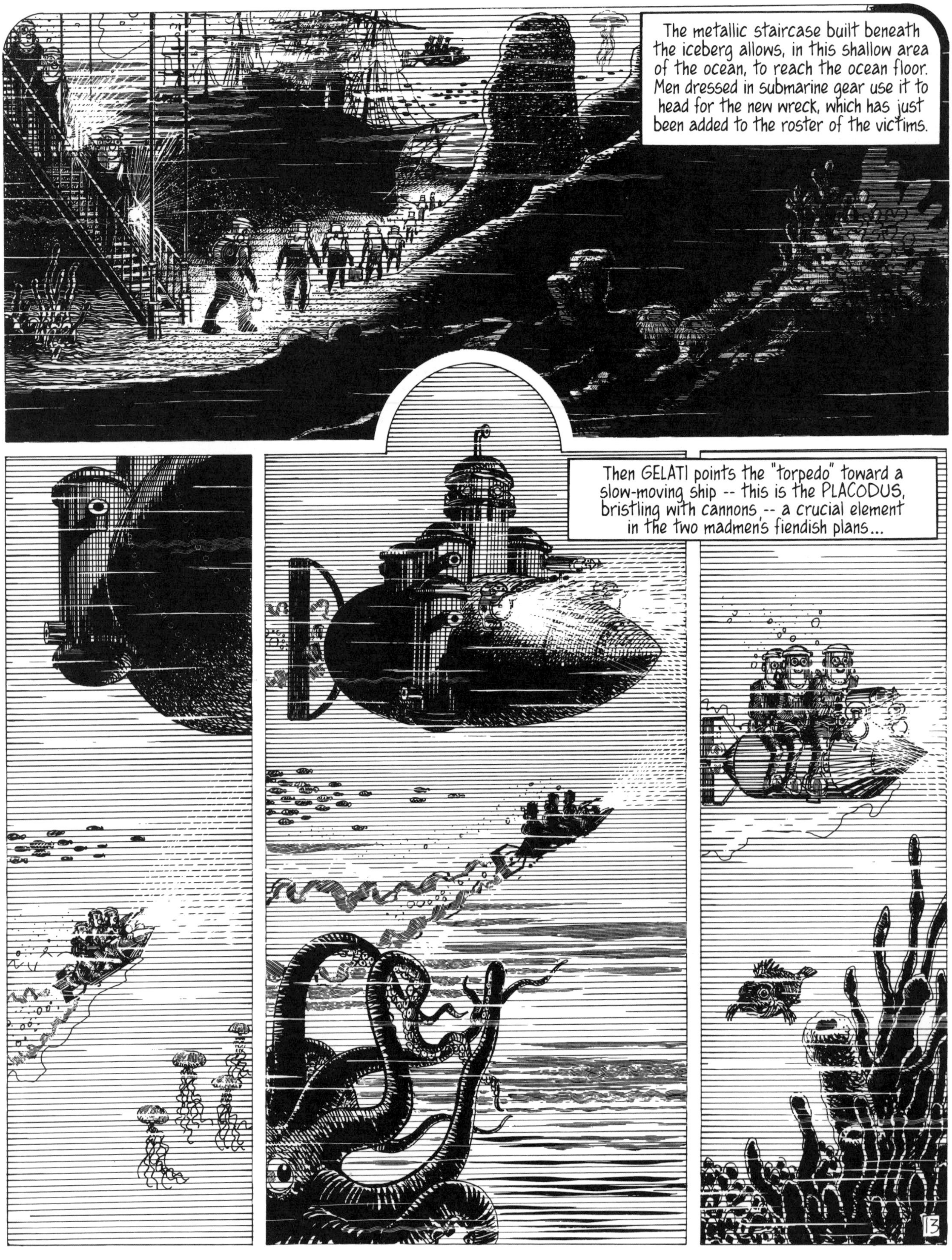
The metallic staircase built beneath the iceberg allows, in this shallow area of the ocean, to reach the ocean floor. Men dressed in submarine gear use it to head for the new wreck, which has just been added to the roster of the victims.
Then GELATI points the "torpedo" toward a slow-moving ship -- this is the PLACODUS, bristling with cannons -- a crucial element in the two madmen's fiendish plans...
13

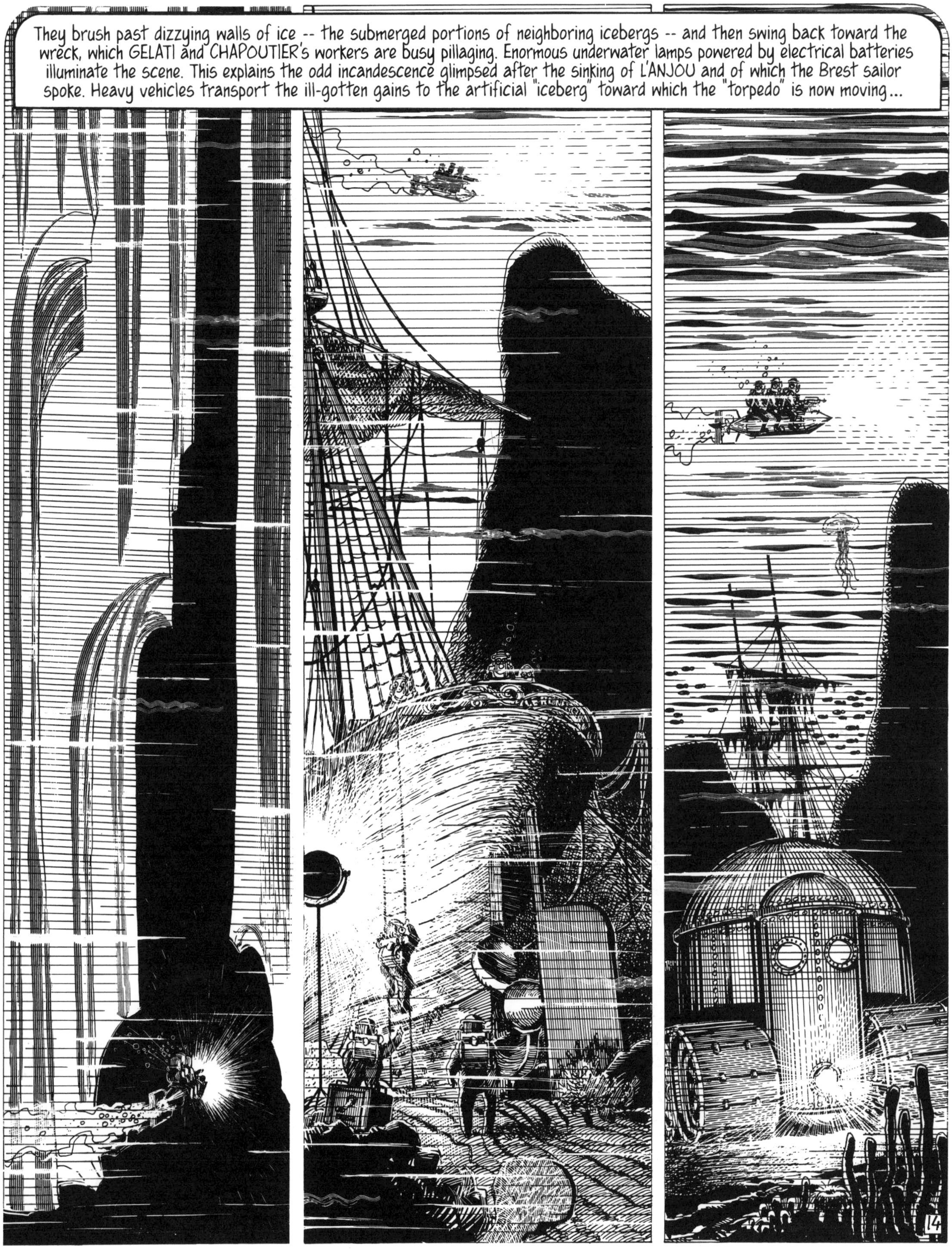
They brush past dizzying walls of ice -- the submerged portions of neighboring icebergs -- and then swing back toward the wreck, which GELATI and CHAPOUTIER's workers are busy pillaging. Enormous underwater lamps powered by electrical batteries illuminate the scene. This explains the odd incandescence glimpsed after the sinking of L'ANJOU and of which the Brest sailor spoke. Heavy vehicles transport the ill-gotten gains to the artificial "iceberg" toward which the "torpedo" is now moving...

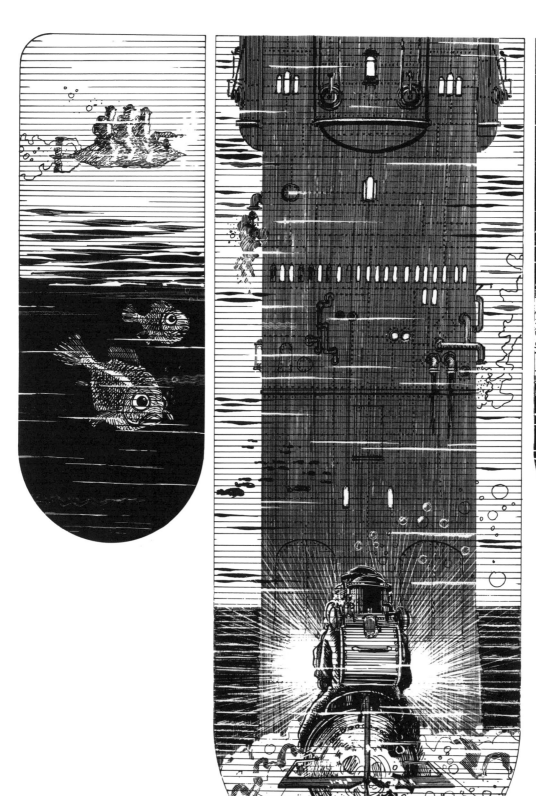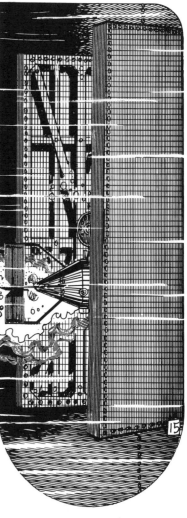

At last they turn back, as the duration for which it is possible to remain underwater is circumscribed. They return to the ARCTIC MARAUDER, whose underwater portion offers itself, magnificent, to the eyes of the three men, symbolizing the excess of the nefarious ambitions of the two madmen. Truly, it has been built to the scale of their madness, for all of its admirable qualities. Oh, if they had only devoted their energies to other pursuits! Is there no one to thwart their wicked plans?

VII

SIMONE POUFFIOT STRIKES!

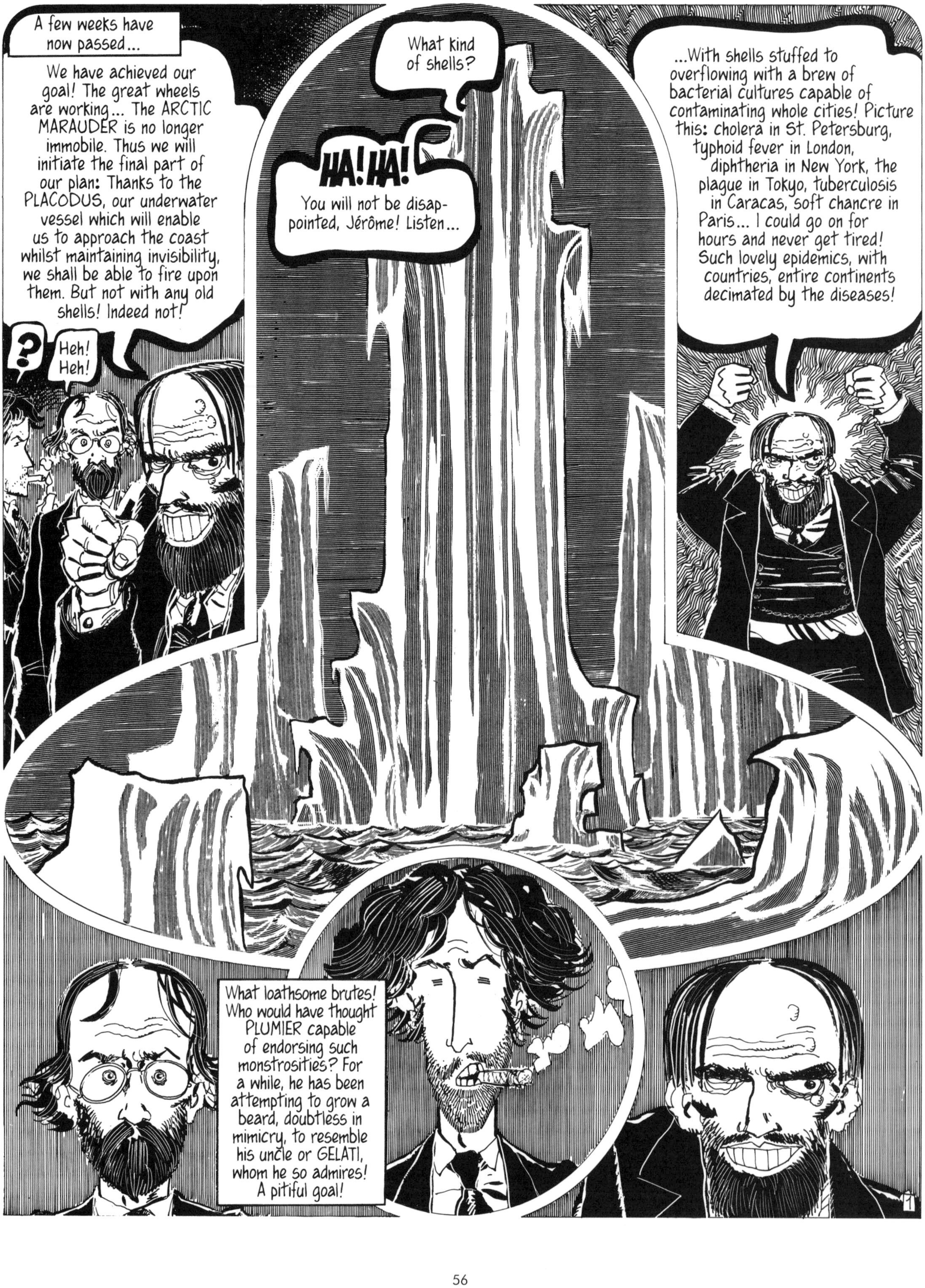
A few weeks have now passed...
We have achieved our goal! The great wheels are working... The ARCTIC MARAUDER is no longer immobile. Thus we will initiate the final part of our plan: Thanks to the PLACODUS, our underwater vessel which will enable us to approach the coast whilst maintaining invisibility, we shall be able to fire upon them. But not with any old shells! Indeed not!
?
Heh! Heh!
What kind of shells?
HA! HA!
You will not be disappointed, Jérôme! Listen...
...With shells stuffed to overflowing with a brew of bacterial cultures capable of contaminating whole cities! Picture this: cholera in St. Petersburg, typhoid fever in London, diphtheria in New York, the plague in Tokyo, tuberculosis in Caracas, soft chancre in Paris... I could go on for hours and never get tired! Such lovely epidemics, with countries, entire continents decimated by the diseases!
What loathsome brutes! Who would have thought PLUMIER capable of endorsing such monstrosities? For a while, he has been attempting to grow a beard, doubtless in mimicry, to resemble his uncle or GELATI, whom he so admires! A pitiful goal!
1

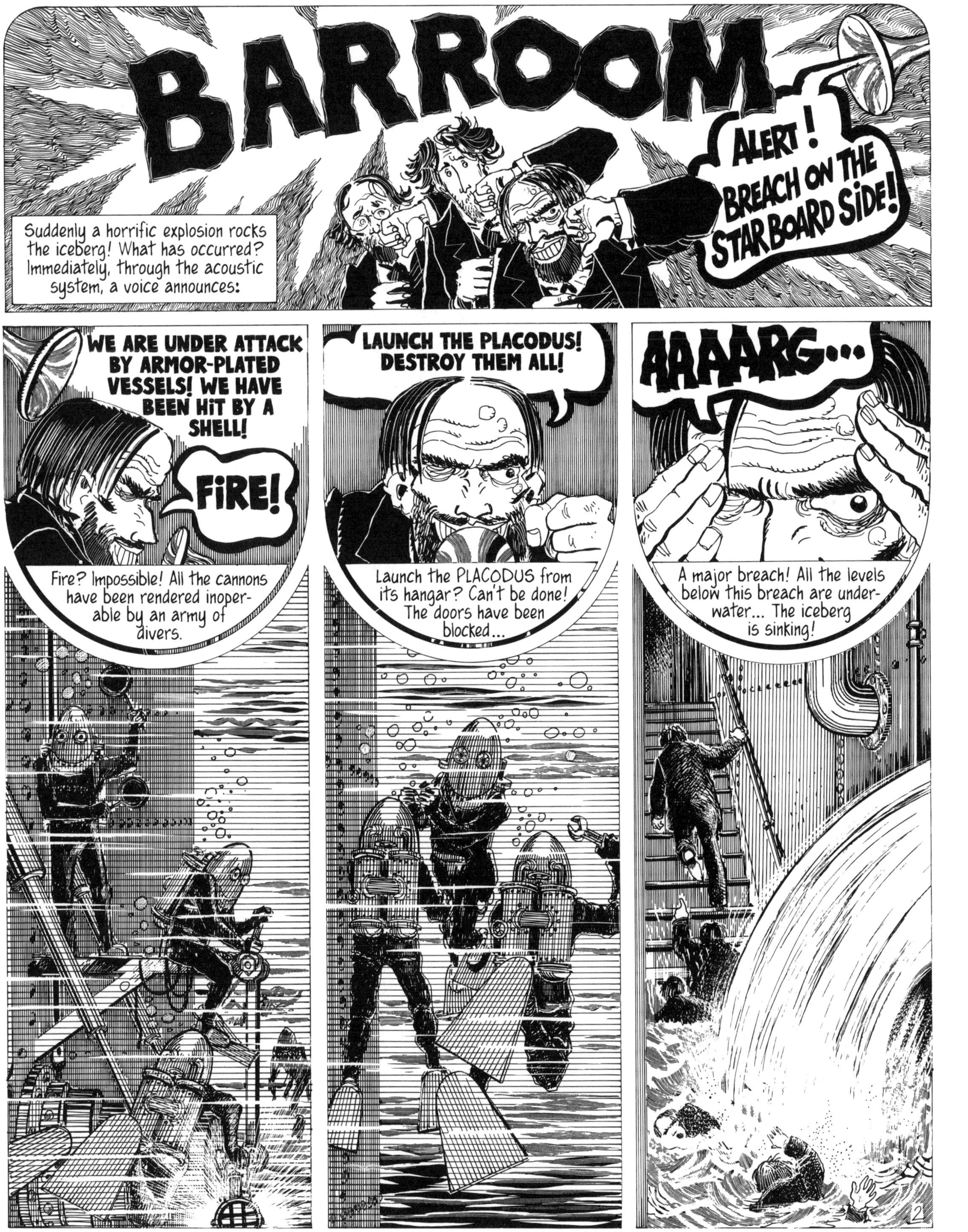
BARROOM
Suddenly a horrific explosion rocks the iceberg! What has occurred? Immediately, through the acoustic system, a voice announces:
ALERT! BREACH ON THE STARBOARD SIDE!
WE ARE UNDER ATTACK BY ARMOR-PLATED VESSELS! WE HAVE BEEN HIT BY A SHELL!
FIRE!
Fire? Impossible! All the cannons have been rendered inoperable by an army of divers.
LAUNCH THE PLACODUS! DESTROY THEM ALL!
Launch the PLACODUS from its hangar? Can't be done! The doors have been blocked...
AAAARG...
A major breach! All the levels below this breach are underwater... The iceberg is sinking!
2

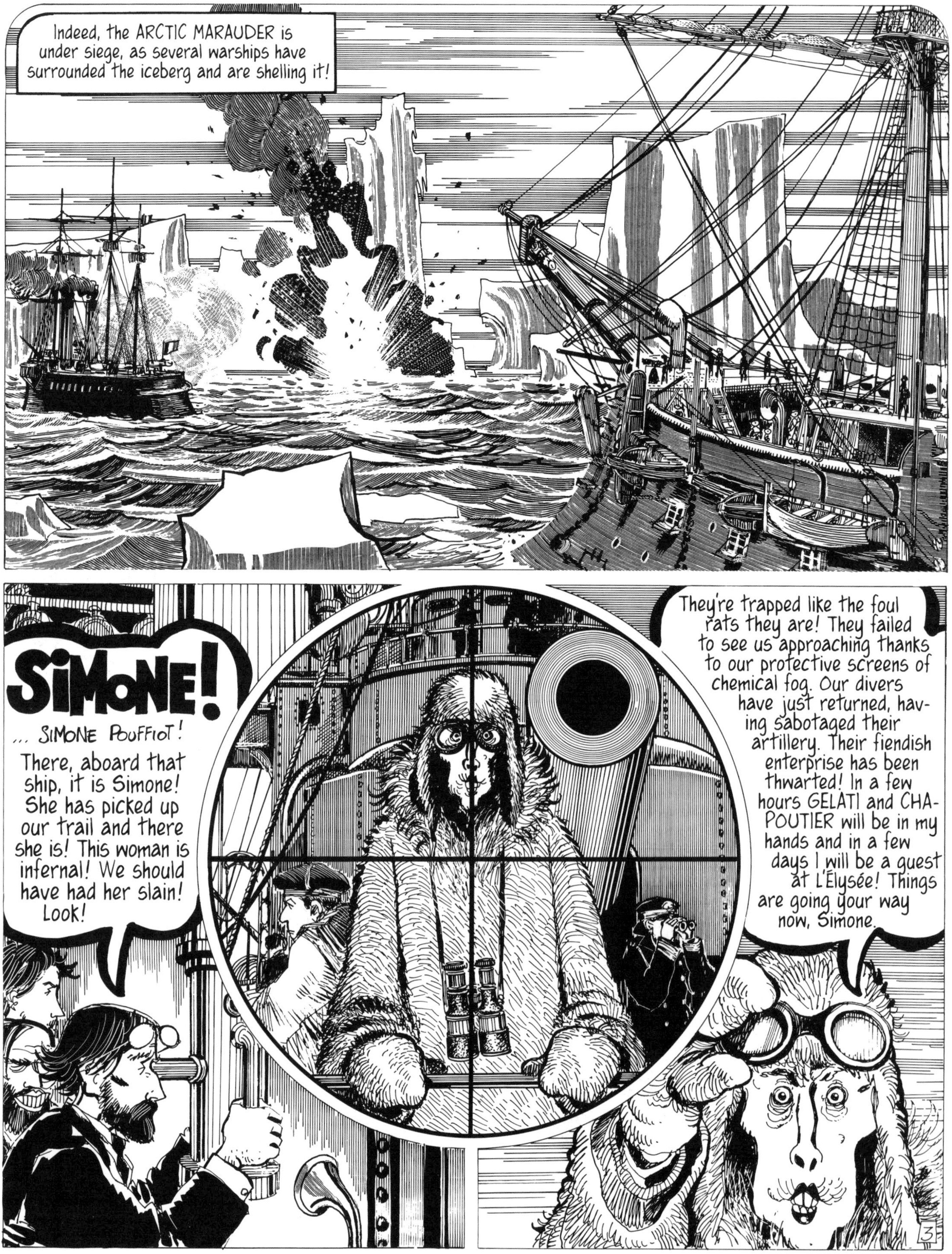
Indeed, the ARCTIC MARAUDER is under siege, as several warships have surrounded the iceberg and are shelling it!
SIMONE! ... SIMONE POUFFIOT! There, aboard that ship, it is Simone! She has picked up our trail and there she is! This woman is infernal! We should have had her slain! Look!
They're trapped like the foul rats they are! They failed to see us approaching thanks to our protective screens of chemical fog. Our divers have just returned, having sabotaged their artillery. Their fiendish enterprise has been thwarted! In a few hours GELATI and CHAPOUTIER will be in my hands and in a few days I will be a guest at L'Élysée! Things are going your way now, Simone.
3

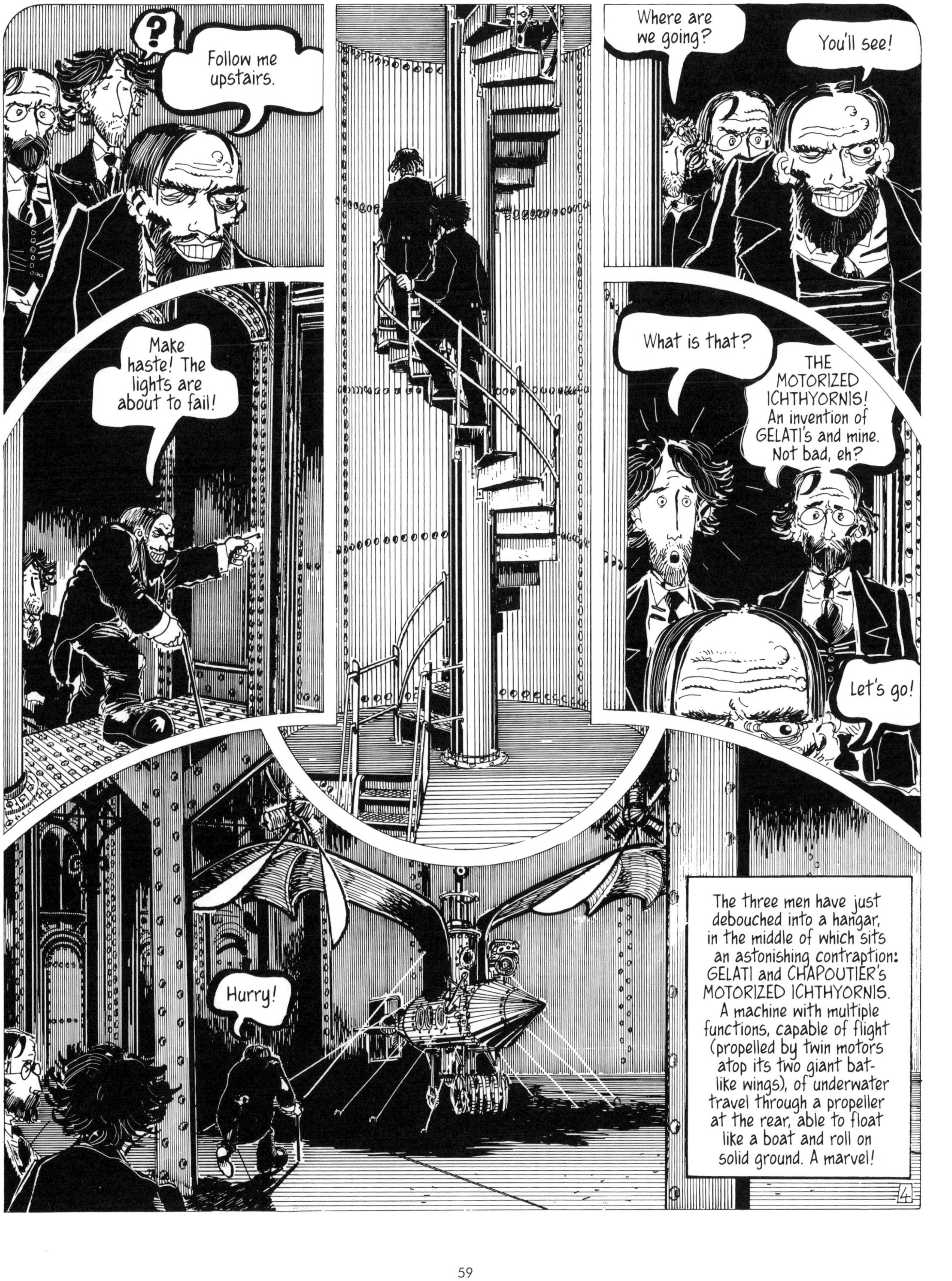
?
Follow me upstairs.
Where are we going?
You'll see!
Make haste! The lights are about to fail!
What is that?
THE MOTORIZED ICHTHYORNIS! An invention of GELATI's and mine. Not bad, eh?
Let's go!
Hurry!
The three men have just debouched into a hangar, in the middle of which sits an astonishing contraption: GELATI and CHAPOUTIER's MOTORIZED ICHTHYORNIS. A machine with multiple functions, capable of flight (propelled by twin motors atop its two giant bat-like wings), of underwater travel through a propeller at the rear, able to float like a boat and roll on solid ground. A marvel!
4

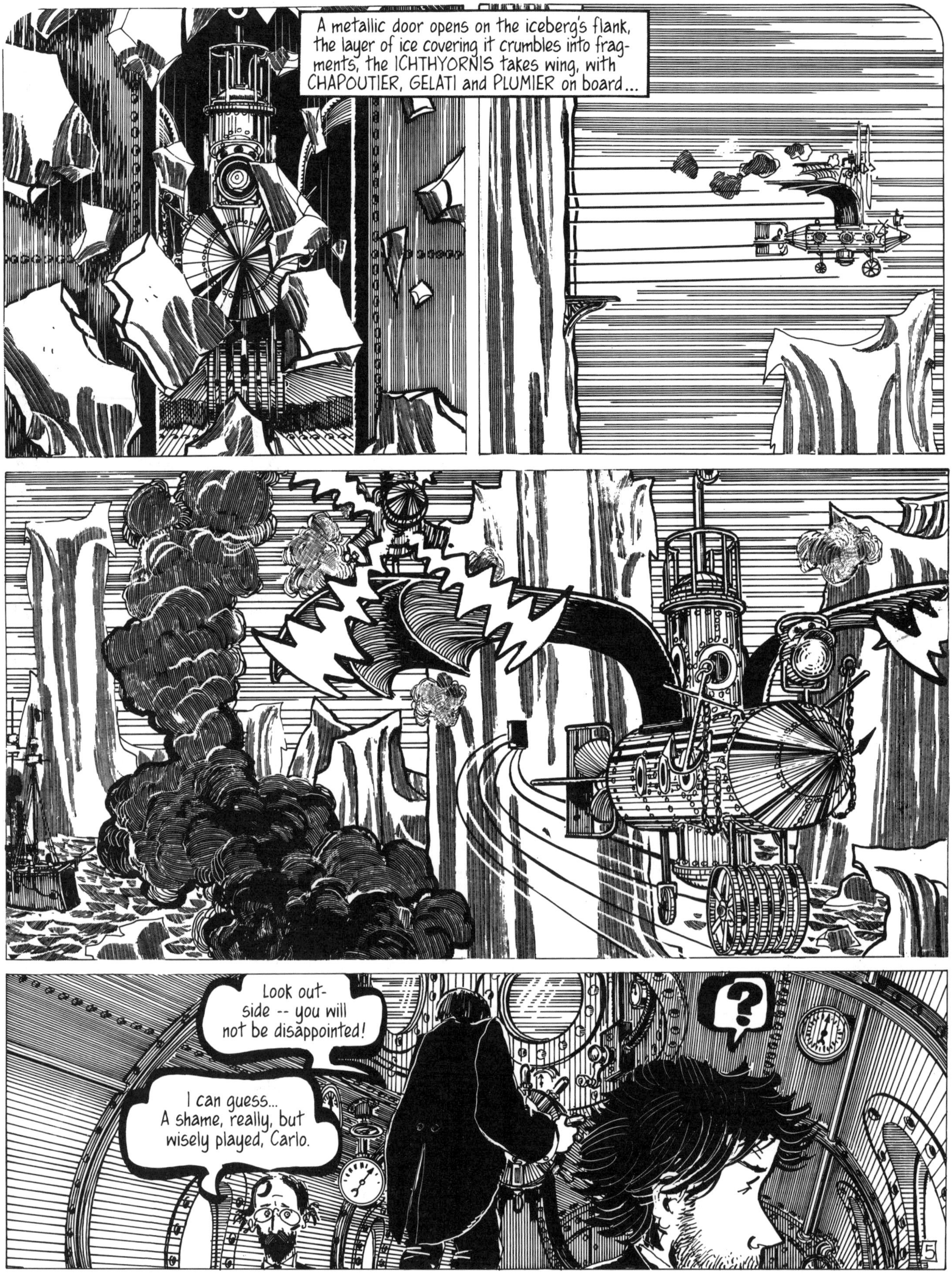
A metallic door opens on the iceberg's flank, the layer of ice covering it crumbles into fragments, the ICHTHYORNIS takes wing, with CHAPOUTIER, GELATI and PLUMIER on board...
Look outside -- you will not be disappointed!
?
I can guess... A shame, really, but wisely played, Carlo.
5

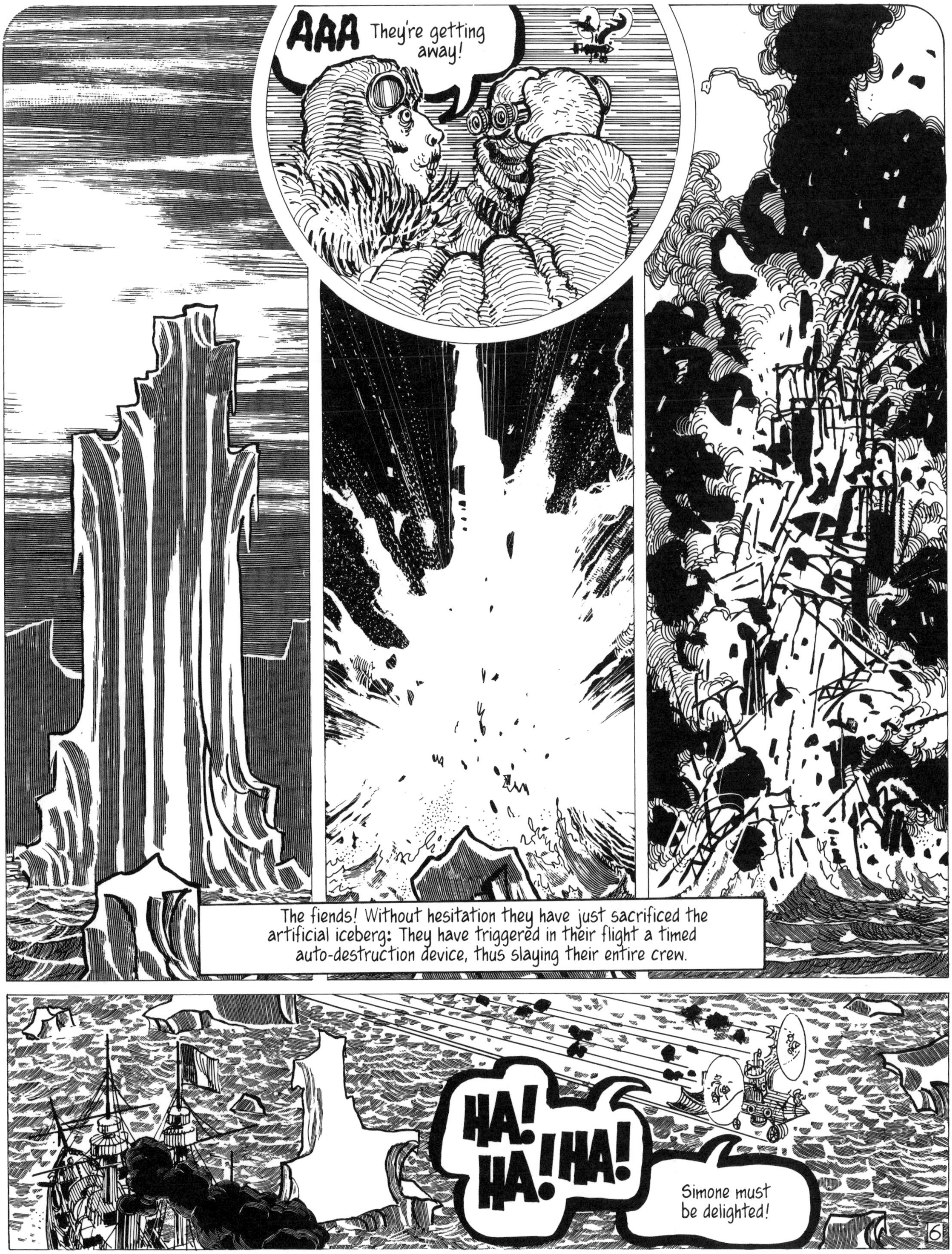
AAA They're getting away!
The fiends! Without hesitation they have just sacrificed the artificial iceberg: They have triggered in their flight a timed auto-destruction device, thus slaying their entire crew.
HA! HA! HA!
Simone must be delighted!
6

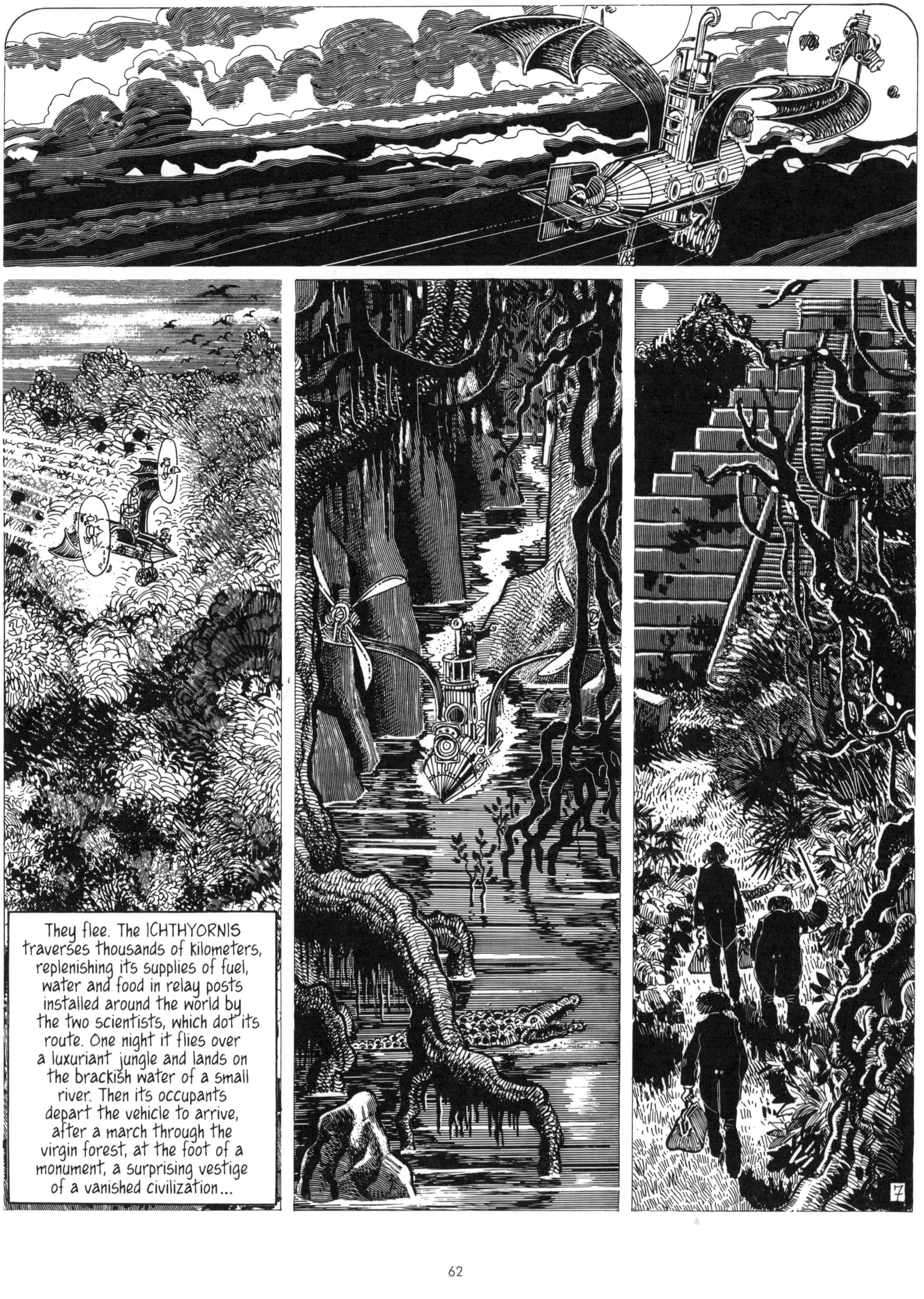
They flee. The ICHTHYORNIS traverses thousands of kilometers, replenishing its supplies of fuel, water and food in relay posts installed around the world by the two scientists, which dot its route. One night it flies over a luxuriant jungle and lands on the brackish water of a small river. Then its occupants depart the vehicle to arrive, after a march through the virgin forest, at the foot of a monument, a surprising vestige of a vanished civilization...
7

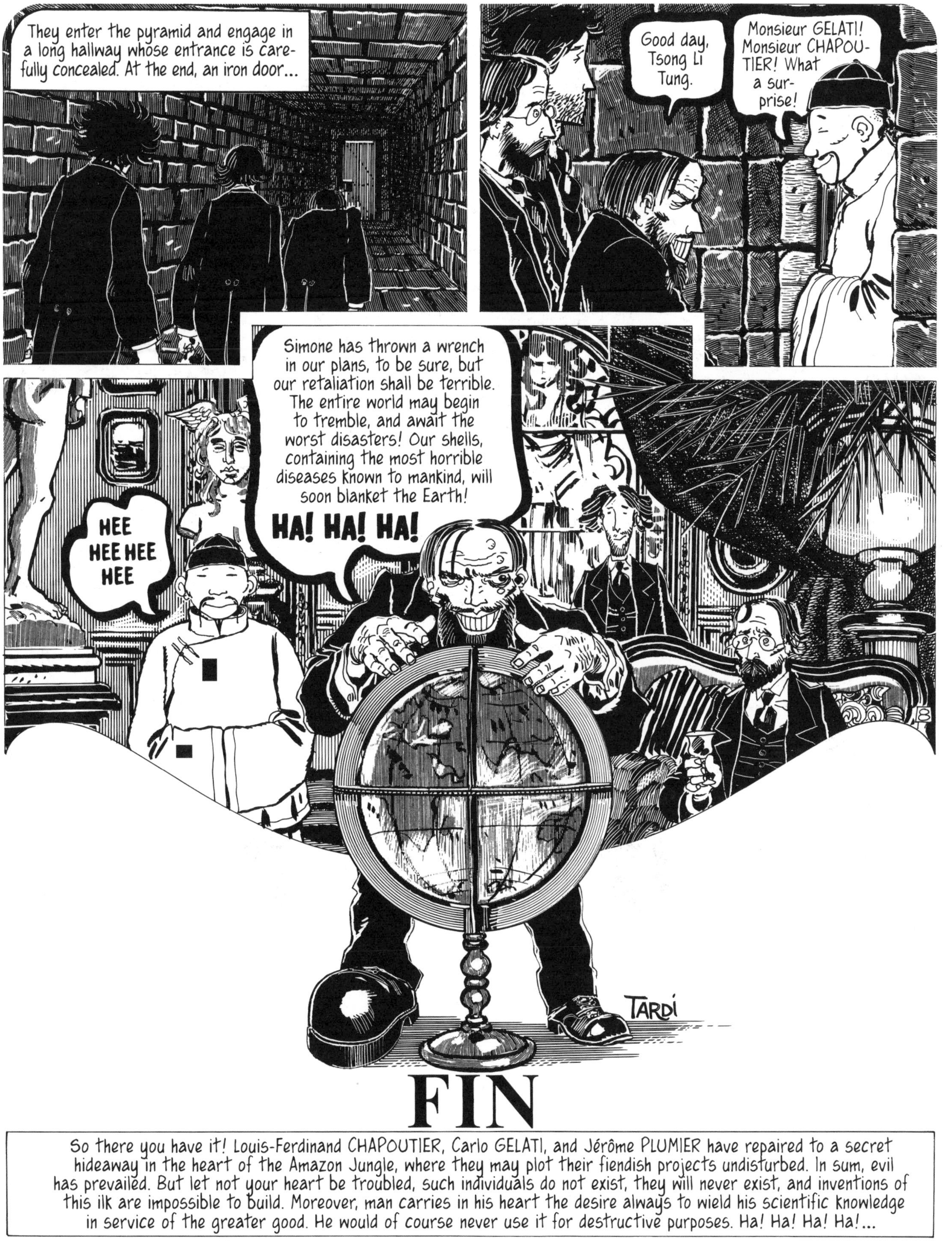
They enter the pyramid and engage in a long hallway whose entrance is carefully concealed. At the end, an iron door...
Good day, Tsong Li Tung.
Monsieur GELATI! Monsieur CHAPOUTIER! What a surprise!
Simone has thrown a wrench in our plans, to be sure, but our retaliation shall be terrible. The entire world may begin to tremble, and await the worst disasters! Our shells, containing the most horrible diseases known to mankind, will soon blanket the Earth!
HA! HA! HA!
HEE HEE HEE HEE
TARDI
FIN

So there you have it! Louis-Ferdinand CHAPOUTIER, Carlo GELATI, and Jérôme PLUMIER have repaired to a secret hideaway in the heart of the Amazon Jungle, where they may plot their fiendish projects undisturbed. In sum, evil has prevailed. But let not your heart be troubled, such individuals do not exist, they will never exist, and inventions of this ilk are impossible to build. Moreover, man carries in his heart the desire always to wield his scientific knowledge in service of the greater good. He would of course never use it for destructive purposes. Ha! Ha! Ha! Ha!...

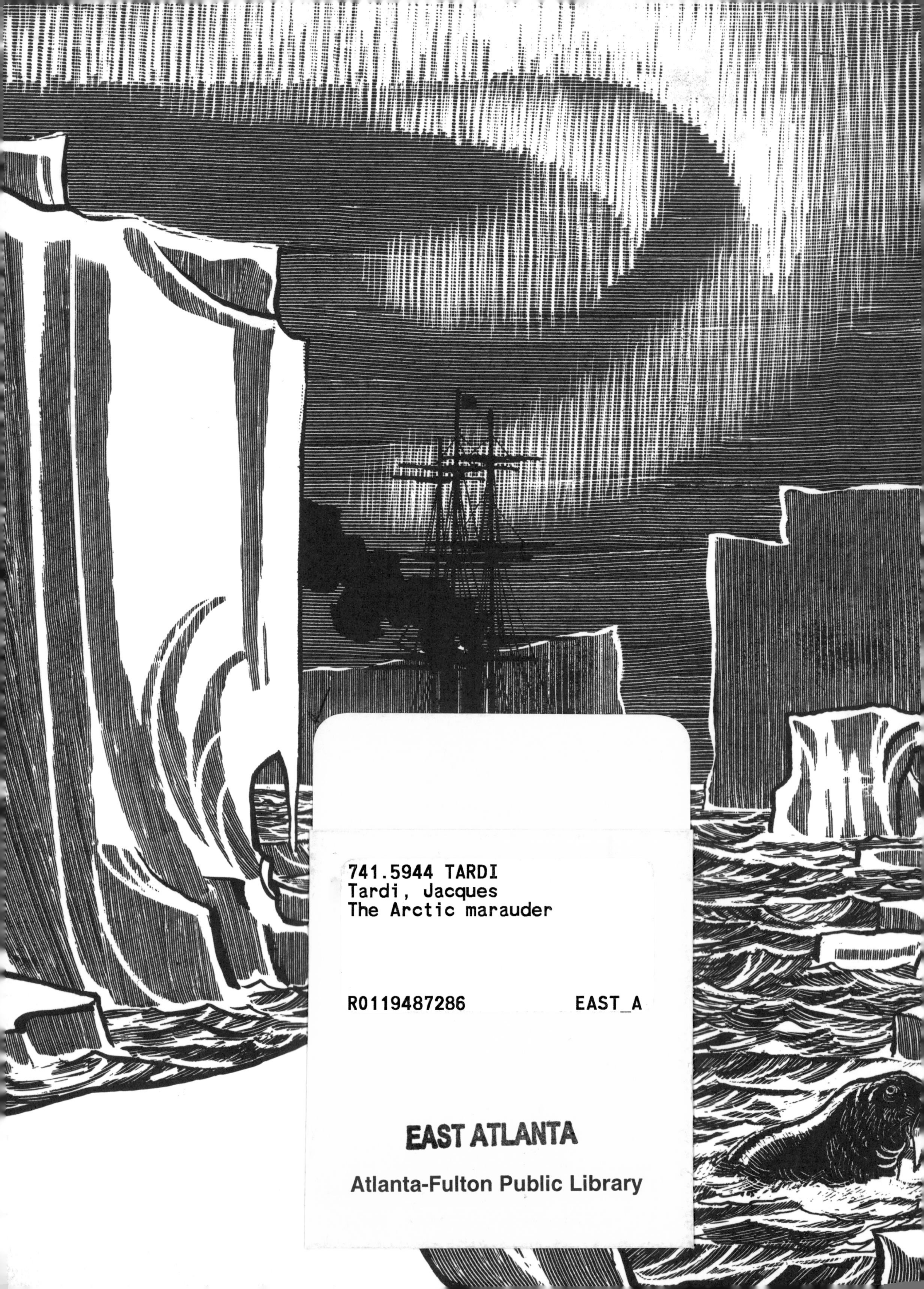